Theatre Royal, Covent-Garden,

This present WEDNESDAY, *April* 12, 1826,

Will be performed *(for the first time)* a Grand Romantic and Fairy OPERA, in three acts, (Founded on WIELAND's celebrated Poem) entitled

OBERON:
OR,
THE ELF-KING's OATH.

With entirely new Music, Scenery, Machinery, Dresses and Decorations.

The OVERTURE and the whole of the MUSIC composed by

CARL MARIA VON WEBER,

Who will preside this Evening in the Orchestra.

The CHORUS (under the direction of Mr. WATSON,) has been greatly augmented.
The DANCES composed by Mr. AUSTIN.
The Scenes painted by Mess. GRIEVE, PUGH, T. and W. GRIEVE, LUPPINO, *and assistants.*
The Machinery by Mr. E. SAUL. The Aerial Machinery, Transformations & Decorations by Mess. BRADWELL
The Dresses by Mr PALMER, Miss EGAN, and assistants.

Fairies.

Oberon, *King of the Fairies*, Mr. C. BLAND,   Puck, Miss H. CAWSE,
Titania, *Queen of the Fairies*, Miss SMITH.

Franks.

Charlemagne, *King of the Franks*, Mr. AUSTIN,
Sir Huon, of Bourdeaux, *Duke of Guienne*,............Mr. BRAHAM,
Sherasmin, *his Squire*,................Mr. FAWCETT,

Arabians.

Haroun-Al-Rashchid, *Caliph of Bagdad*, Mr. CHAPMAN,
Baba-Khan, *a Saracenic Prince*, Mr. BAKER,   Hassan, *Master of a Vessel*, Mr. J. ISAACS,
Hamet, Mr. EVANS,   Amrou, M`ATKINS,
Reiza, *Daughter of the Caliph*,..........Miss PATON,
Fatima, Madame VESTRIS,
Namouna, *Fatima's Grandmother*, Mrs. DAVENPORT.

Tunisians.

Almansor, *Emir of Tunis*,......Mr. COOPER,
Abdallah, *a Corsair*, Mr. HORREBOW,   Slave, Mr. TINNEY,
Roshana, *Wife of Almansor*,..........Miss LACY,
Nadina, *a female Slave*, Mrs. WILSON.
Officers, Soldiers, Slaves, &c. of the different Courts,——Fairies, Sprites, &c.

Order of the Scenery:

OBERON'S BOWER,

With the VISION.   *Painted by Mr. Grieve.*
Distant View of Bagdad, and the adjacent Country on the Banks of the Tigris,
By Sunset.   Grieve
INTERIOR of NAMOUNA's COTTAGE,   T. Grieve
VESTIBULE and TERRACE in the HAREM of the CALIPH, overlooking the Tigris. W. Grieve
GRAND BANQUETTING CHAMBER of HAROUN. T. Grieve

GARDENS of the PALACE.   Pugh
PORT OF ASCALON.   T. Grieve
RAVINE amongst the ROCKS of a DESOLATE ISLAND,
The Haunt of the Spirits of the Storm.   Designed by Bradwell, and painted by Pugh.

Perforated Cavern on the Beach,

With the OCEAN—in a STORM—a CALM—by SUNSET—
*Twilight—Starlight—*and *Moonlight.*   T. Grieve

Exterior of Gardener's House in the Pleasure Grounds of the Emir of Tunis. Grieve
Hall and Gallery in Almansor's Palace.   W. Grieve
MYRTLE GROVE in the GARDENS of the EMIR.   Pugh
GOLDEN SALOON in the KIOSK of ROSHANA.   W. Grieve.
The Palace and Gardens, by Moonlight.   Grieve.
COURT of the HAREM.   Pugh.
HALL of ARMS in the Palace of Charlemagne. Grieve & Luppino

The Opera is published, & may be had in the Theatre, & of Mess. Hunt & Clarke, 38, Tavistock-street, Covent-Garden

To which will be added (23d time) a NEW PIECE, in one act, called

THE SCAPE-GOAT.

Old Eustace,   Mr. BLANCHARD,   Charles,   Mr. COOPER,
Ignatius Polyglot,   Mr. W. FARREN,   Robin,   Mr. MEADOWS,
Molly Maggs,   Miss JONES,   Harriet,   Miss A. JONES.

W. REYNOLDS, Printer, 9. Denmark-Court Strand

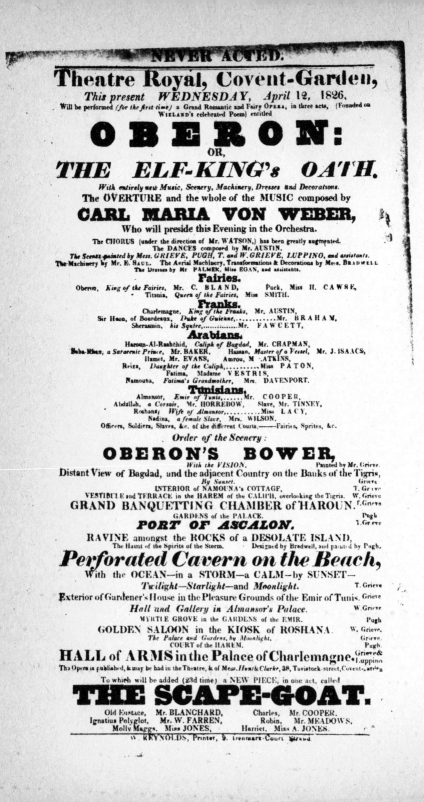

OBERON
OLD AND NEW

Anthony Burgess

Hutchinson
London Melbourne Sydney Auckland Johannesburg

Hutchinson & Co. (Publishers) Ltd

An imprint of Century Hutchinson Limited

Brookmount House, 62–65 Chandos Place, London WC2N 4NW

Hutchinson Publishing Group (Australia) Pty Ltd
16–22 Church Street, Hawthorn, Melbourne, Victoria 3122

Hutchinson Group (NZ) Ltd
32–34 View Road, PO Box 40–086, Glenfield, Auckland 10

Hutchinson Group (SA) Pty Ltd
PO Box 337, Bergvlei 2012, South Africa

First published 1985
Introduction and Burgess's Oberon © Anthony Burgess 1985

Set in Linotron Bembo by
Input Typesetting Ltd, London

Printed and bound in Great Britain by
REDWOOD BURN LIMITED
Trowbridge, Wiltshire

ISBN 0 09 163521 7

INTRODUCTION

The playbill for the first performance of Weber's *Oberon* is still extant. It seems to advertise more of a Christmas pantomime than a grand opera, drawing attention to marvellous transformation scenes – from the 'Ravine amongst the Rocks of a Desolate Island, the Haunt of the Spirits of the Storm' to a 'Perforated Cavern on the Beach, With the Ocean – in a Storm – a Calm – by Sunset – *Twilight* – *Starlight* – and *Moonlight*' ending with the 'Hall of Arms in the Palace of Charlemagne'. There are fairies, Franks, Arabians and Tunisians, as also Carl Maria von Weber, 'who will preside this Evening in the Orchestra'. It was not, however, a Boxing Day occasion but a spring one – the date was 12 April 1826. The venue was the Theatre Royal, Covent Garden.

Weber not only conducted; he appeared on the stage afterwards to be applauded, though the greater part of the applause went to the scenery and stage effects. He was very ill and had been told by his doctors that he had little time left to live. One of his motives in accepting a commission to set an English opera libretto by the poetaster James Robinson Planché, and to rehearse and conduct the resulting work in London, was to earn some money for a family which was soon to be widowed and orphaned. Death came sooner than even he expected – on 5 June 1826, the day before he proposed returning to Germany. He was buried in Moorfields Chapel amid great public mourning, for Londoners had learned to love him as a man as well as to admire him as a musician. In 1844 Richard Wagner arranged for the coffin to be transferred to Dresden. There he now lies. He was very much a German composer, and a great one. But he had composed an opera we have to call English, even though few have ever seen it performed in England.

Of course, we all know the Overture, one of the world's

favourites, and there used to be concert performances of Reiza's great aria 'Ocean, thou mighty monster'. But the work as a whole remains unknown – apart from long-playing records of the constituent numbers – because of the mediocrity of the libretto. And even if we could stomach Planché's bad blank verse – the words for the arias are tolerable; they are swallowed by the exquisite settings – we could not now afford the pantomime stage effects. If you ask what blank verse is doing in an opera, you have to remember that *Oberon* is closer to *The Magic Flute*, which the Germans call a *Singspiel*, than to what Weber regarded as true opera, with its sung recitatives. When he first encountered Planché's libretto he was filled with anxiety: this was not the kind of thing he was used to; nevertheless he went ahead and wasted ravishing music on a rather childish extravaganza. *Oberon* is just one of innumerable examples of operas which fail to get into the repertory because of the unacceptability of the libretto.

The libretto of *Oberon* is based on Sotheby's translation of a poem by Wieland, and the poem itself is based on the medieval story of Huon of Bordeaux, a knight of Charlemagne's court who undergoes a trial of love at the hands of the King of the Fairies. Oberon (or Auberon – a name probably of Frankish origin) is thus seen not to be an invention of Shakespeare's but a well-established myth. Puck, however, who has his part in the opera, is lifted straight from Shakespeare. The story as Planché tells it goes something like this. Oberon and Titania his queen have quarrelled and parted in anger, and they swear 'Never to meet in love till some fond pair, through weal and woe, 'mid flood, chains, and fire should keep their plighted faith inviolate.' Puck tells Oberon that Sir Huon has incurred the wrath of Charlemagne by slaying his son, though in self-defence, and has been commanded to go to the Caliph's Hall in Baghdad, slay whoever sits on the right hand of the Caliph, Haroun al Raschid, and then claim his daughter as his bride. Oberon here sees an opportunity of sending a 'fond pair' through the trials of flood and fire. First, though, Huon and the Caliph's daughter Reiza have to be made to fall in love with each other. This is accomplished by means of a two-way television device, whereby Reiza and Huon see each other and are equally and heavily smitten.

Led by duty and desire, Huon goes off to Baghdad. To
help him in his double mission Oberon gives him a magic
horn, to be sounded whenever danger is too great to be
overcome by ordinary human strength and cunning. Then
Oberon's magic will step in. Huon has not only a horn but
a comic squire, Sherasmin. Reiza has a female attendant called
Fatima. These make up a convenient operatic quartet – tenor,
baritone, soprano and mezzo. The four get away from the
court of Haroun and board a ship bound for Greece. But
things are not to be made too easy for them. Puck raises a
colossal storm and the four are shipwrecked. Pirates come
along, knock Huon down and make off with Reiza, Sherasmin and Fatima to Tunis, where the lighter half of the
quartet settle to a life of slavery. But Oberon helps Huon to
follow them. In Tunis Huon hears that Reiza has been
presented as a possible bride to the Emir. He gets into the
harem, seeking her, but meets instead Roshana, wife of the
Emir, who requests the white knight to kill her husband and
accept her love as a reward. The Emir enters the harem, is
full of wrath at the sight of Huon and orders that he be burnt
at the stake, dog of a Christian. Reiza asks to be burnt with
him, and this request is graciously granted. But the magic
horn is blown, Oberon appears and says that they have
suffered enough, their trials are over and they have come
through them very satisfactorily. The fairy king and queen
are reconciled and Huon proceeds in triumph, mission
accomplished, to the court of Charlemagne.

This is a reasonable piece of melodrama by the standards
of the early nineteenth century – which loved Islamic
monsters and ruthless pirates – but it is very difficult to
accept Planché's verse, of which the following is a fair
specimen (Oberon is speaking):

> Peace, varlet! Hear me, Paladin.
> Relentless Charlemagne would have thy blood;
> But thou shalt execute his dread command,
> And to thy native France triumphantly
> Bear back thy beauteous bride; rest thou but true
> Amidst the trials fate prepares for thee.
> Therefore receive, Sir Duke, this magic horn;
> Whatever danger may thy path beset,
> Its slightest sound will bring thee sudden aid;

Need'st thou the presence of the fairy king,
A bolder blast will bring me to thy side,
Tho' planets roll between us.

This is not exactly Shakespearean.

I was asked by the Scottish National Opera Company to do something about providing a libretto more acceptable to modern taste. I found it was not possible to discard totally the original Planché story, for the elementary reason that the opera is called *Oberon* and has to remain *Oberon*: it would be unseemly to have a work called *Jack Robinson* or *A Bed for Sundered Lovers* – music by Weber, text by Burgess; there would be too many explanations to give. So *Oberon* the opera remains, which means that Oberon has to be in the cast. This means fairies and also Puck, whom Shakespeare has consecrated as Oberon's right-hand goblin. Oberon's magic horn is not only in the text; it is also in the music and establishes itself in the very first bars of the Overture. The thing to do, I thought, was to accept ironically the fairy-magic furniture and make the characters aware of it as inherited luggage which, despite their modern scepticism, they have to accept because they know they are performing in an opera. This is known, I believe, as the Alienation Effect.

For the characters are modern, and the heroic four are even American, which makes them very modern. The circumstances they find themselves in connect rather gruesomely with those of Planché's libretto. At this very instant of writing, Islamic skyjackers are holding Christian and Jewish Americans to ransom. It did not require much imagination on my part to change Planché's Baghdad to a kind of modern Teheran, where a couple of American girls are being held hostage and American emissaries have to buy them out of bondage with cash from Washington. The use of Oberon's horn to procure release remains fanciful, but we can always rationalize this to our sceptical satisfaction by invoking the scientifically established effect of high upper partials on human nervous systems. But the story remains a fairy one: it would be totally impermissible to turn Oberon into a mere clever and benevolent mortal.

You can call this a comic opera, though the music does not suggest Offenbach or Sir Arthur Sullivan. It is serious

music and much of it is very beautiful. We can only justify
putting it into the larynxes of comic characters by calling on
a certain distancing effect. Reiza (now Rezia) can sing what
has become 'Ocean, you mighty monster' (still a tribute to
Planché) because she has been a member of an amateur operatic society set up, improbably, by the American Embassy
in Teheran (or wherever it is). All the members of the quartet
are conscious of the orchestra down there in the pit and they
know the score as characters, not as actors playing characters.
There is even an unworthy reference to the fags in the
orchestra – first and second fags or fagotti or bassoons. There
is a good deal of facetiousness, but this is because the main
personages are modern non-intellectual Americans. Laughs
are deliberately played for, which they were not – much –
in Planché, who would today provoke the wrong kind of
laughter.

In putting new words to the arias and choruses, I was
amazed at the care Weber had taken to get the stresses of the
English right. We know that, always the thorough
professional, he worked hard at English before setting
Planché, but the scrupulousness with which he approaches
natural English speech stress is quite remarkable – especially
when we think of Stravinsky's cavalier approach to it, or
even that of certain pop composers who have the advantage
of thinking they know English as a first language. Behind
my own words, in aria and ensemble, there has to be the
ghost of Planché, because Weber was listening with great
care to his very respectable prosody. The diction, I think, is
another matter, but I make no great claim for my own. The
important thing is to reinstate, after a too long silence, a very
beautiful and moving score. My words bow down to it.

OBERON

A Fantastic Opera

Libretto by Anthony Burgess

(WITH ACKNOWLEDGEMENTS TO
JAMES ROBINSON PLANCHÉ)

Music by Carl Maria von Weber

CHARACTERS

Oberon and Titania, guardians of the natural order
Puck, their assistant
Hugh and Geoffrey, test pilots
Rezia and Selina, former secretaries in a Western embassy
in the Muslim state of Naraka
Harun, ruler of Naraka
Lot, his Westernized brother
President of the U-S-

Roblets
Houris
Muslim police
Troops
Thugs
The Elements
Mermaids
Fairies
Elves
U-S- citizens

Overture

Towards the end of the Overture it is conceivable that we might see, in dumb show, OBERON *and* TITANIA *violently quarrelling. She goes off in anger. He is left alone, wretched, and eventually lies down to rest. The weird assistants of* OBERON *come softly on and assemble in various portions of the stage.*

ACT ONE

The place is a mysterious one, science-fiction-like, with strange shifting shadows, angular, not at all natural. OBERON, *who combines in his appearance the insect and animal and human, is now asleep on a couch of very curious cut. The creatures, whom we will call* ROBLETS, *sing.*

No. 1 *Lullaby*

ROBLETS:
 Still the air, the light be dim.
 Let no care alight on him.
 Loud the silent world without,
 Even though we shut it out.
 Muffle the mosquito's din,
 Keep that bee from buzzing in.
 Sound asleep lies Oberon:
 Rest at last has bound him fast.
 Slumber on till pain is gone,
 Wake to find the past is past.
 No. Even he and even we
 Know all too well what must be must be.
 Sleep sleep sleep sleep.
 Though sadly we and sadly he
 Know all too well that what must be must be.

PUCK *comes in, misshapen and ugly, a real hobgoblin.*

PUCK: What goes on here?

A ROBLET: He's asleep now, sir. We were just watching over him.

PUCK: A bit too vocally, if I may say so. I know – this is an opera and there are certain conventions. Off – you have things to do. Dripping dew into daisies and so on. Painting freckles on the throats of cowslips. But, of course, that's a little out of date. Off – do something.

They go, rather noisily.

PUCK (*to the audience*): You know me – Puck. You know him – Oberon. We've met before – under different circumstances. Things have changed. No fairies nowadays. Regard us as guardians of the natural order, aspects of the ecology. But some things don't change all that much. Oberon still represents the male principle of the universe. Titania, his wife, who's locked herself in her dressing room, is the eternal female. Like all married couples they quarrel sometimes. This time they've quarrelled over fidelity. Titania said that no male was ever faithful – at least not for long. Oberon said: how about females? Then the general became the particular. A real regular row. Titania went off, screaming that she'd come back only when he – he – he had found a pair of lovers who stayed faithful under the most impossible circumstances. There's a certain lack of logic somewhere. Oberon is really more worried than she is. He knows that the stability of the universe depends on the harmony of the yin and the yang – or the Oberonic and the Titanian. She knows it too but she forgets it sometimes. Oberon fears earthquakes, universal famine, planetary collisions, acid rain. He wants her back. He needs her. You need them both. I can help, I think. Still, let him sleep a little. And when he wakes he won't find me here. Not at first. There are some things it's unpleasant to see as soon as you wake up. I gather I'm one of them.

He flits off clumsily, being a hobgoblin. OBERON *painfully wakes and sings.*

No. 2 Aria

OBERON: Sleep no more. A nightmare hovers
             Best confronted in the light.
             Yet this pain of sundered lovers
             Is no phantom of the night.
             Princes who sustain creation
             Blast creation with their eyes
             When those eyes flash desolation.
             Nature droops and nature dies.
             Sleep no more.

OBERON (*calling*):   Puck! Puck!

PUCK *looks in cautiously*.

OBERON: My gentle Puck, come hither.

PUCK: That, sir, is the wrong play. (*He approaches* OBERON.)

OBERON: I trust you've been putting forty-minute girdles round about the earth – in my desperate service.

PUCK: Yes – satellitic, that's me. I think I've found what you need, sir. A young man named Hugh. Pure Caucasian. He's in love with a girl of Italian extraction called Rezia. Short for Lucrezia. Lucretia, Lucrece – a chaste Roman matron, you remember.

OBERON: I remember her well. She was – tarquinized.

PUCK: There's a Muslim theocracy where they took Western hostages three years ago. Their deposed emperor had money in Western banks. Their new head says that that money belongs to the state. He took hostages from the Western embassies. Most of the money was released, and so were most of the hostages. But there's a sum outstanding and two hostages as well. Rezia and her friend Selina. Secretaries in one of the Western embassies. The chief Harun, a sort of ayatollah, gives three more days for the outstanding payment. Otherwise the girls will be – well –

OBERON: Tarquinized?

PUCK: Oh, much worse. A pity. They're good innocent girls. Members of an amateur operatic group. They're not singing now. You can see Rezia – she's under televisual surveillance. I have the code number here. Rather a long one.

OBERON *takes from* PUCK *a large dry beechleaf. He approaches a great screen and activates the dials, following the number on the beechleaf.* REZIA *appears. She is dark-haired and ravishing, and she strums a guitar.*

PUCK: Sorry, I was wrong. There are some singers you can't stop singing.

No. 3 Arietta

REZIA: If only my sighing
           Were strong as my fear,
           My sighs would go flying
           To ears that must hear.
           Soon darkness will cover
           My hopes and my all.
           I call on my lover –
           Oh, come to my call.

OBERON *switches her image off. He consults* PUCK*'s beechleaf.*

OBERON: So. She's locked up in a prison in the city of Kinching in the Islamic state of Naraka. But where is this –

PUCK: Hugh? At his work in the great Western federation where most of the disputed money was banked. A test pilot or some such thing. They met at an embassy party when he was delivering an aircraft for the deposed ruler – they fell in love. Foolish mortals. Since this business started he's been trying everything to get her out. Disguise. Forged visas. Flying in but always buzzed away by Sumac fighters. He's desperate. It looks to me like true love.

OBERON: We'd better bring him here. Do you have the coordinates?

PUCK: Certainly, sir. (*He hands over another beechleaf.*) He has a colleague with him – Geoffrey, nice but not bright. Rather superstitious.

OBERON: Let's have them both.

He works at a kind of pocket computer. Lights flicker and change. Two shimmering male figures appear in flying uniform. Unshimmering, they look about them, bewildered. They are HUGH *and* GEOFFREY.

HUGH: What is this? Where am I?

GEOFFREY: We, he means.

OBERON: Nothing to fear, gentlemen of the earth, air.
You're in the presence of Oberon – known to the ignorant
as the Fairy King. Now we have a more resounding title
– Half-Sustainer of the Cosmos. The other half being my
consort Titania. Unfortunately not with us at the moment.

GEOFFREY: Fairies –

OBERON: *Not* fairies.

GEOFFREY: But I always liked the idea of fairies. My hands
used to be red-raw with clapping when, you know, Tinker
Bell was in trouble.

PUCK: Tinker Bell – ugh –

HUGH: How did we get here?

PUCK: Teleportation. You've read about it in books. Puck.

HUGH: Pardon me?

PUCK: Puck. They call me Puck.

HUGH: Why are we here?

OBERON: To be helped. We know all about your anguish
over the situation of the woman you love. Today you fly
to her.

HUGH: I've tried it before. It won't work.

OBERON: This time it will.

GEOFFREY: I go too?

OBERON: There are two passages booked.

GEOFFREY: So I go east. I was never farther east than
Hamburg.

OBERON: You'll meet opposition, of course. That's why I
give you this instrument. (*A horn is handed up from the
orchestra.*) Thank you. It looks like a horn. It sounds like
a horn. But the upper harmonics induce instant paralysis
– it lasts about three hours. The horn needs rest after this
exertion. Twenty-four hours, to be exact. Plug your ears
when you sound it. Get your loved one and her friend to
do the same. Blow it fortissimo and I shall be with you
in person. But you can only do that once.

HUGH: What can I say?

OBERON: Sing instead. We'll all sing.

HUGH (*as the prelude sounds*):   This music sounds, you know, early nineteenth-century. Beethoven? No, not clumsy enough.

OBERON: An earthling called Carl Maria von Weber. Ah, here comes the chorus –

The ROBLETS *trot in. All sing.*

No. 4 Ensemble

CHORUS:
> Courage and skill bring you grace and renown.
> We add to your gifts a miraculous crown
> Withheld from the coward, the cur and the clown,
> Whom goblins benight and fright strikes down.

HUGH:
> Guide me to my chosen goal,
> Where a tyrant oppresses decent men.
> There let the steel re-invest my soul.
> Then O then let me kiss her again.

OBERON:
> Without the aid of my new techniques
> This great scheme we entertain
> Could not accomplish itself in days or weeks,
> And the toughest of male physiques
> Would crack beneath the strain.
> But look – the transformation's done:
> You greet an alien sun.

OBERON, PUCK *and the* CHORUS *have withdrawn into a penumbra during the above.* HUGH *and* GEOFFREY *seem to have been placed in a module whizzing rapidly over the moon and stars. They seem to drop down to view a distant panorama – sky, city, river.*

GEOFFREY:
> What will science think of next?

HUGH:
> All my senses stand perplexed.
> No – I can't believe my eyes –
> Crystal city all aquiver,
> Shivering quartz and amarinthine skies.

There is the gold-and-silver-burning river.
But where do we start seeking?
My love, dear face, imprinted on my heart for ever,
Hidden in what turquoise tower,
Dead to all my skill's endeavour?

OBERON:

Be bold. Breathe deep. Take heart.
Here's reason reason freely gives –
He holds her in his power
And that must mean: she lives.

HUGH:

Guide me now to my chosen goal
Where the tyrant maintains his sway.
There let iron steel my soul,
There let me steal my dear love away.
Let me rain upon her brow, sweetly on her brow,
Kisses that stamp an unbreakable vow.
Let me press upon her lips and on her brow
Kisses sweet and strong,
Signals of love that has languished too long,
Kisses on her lips and on her brow,
Kisses sweet and strong.
Guide my journey – I start it now.

CHORUS (*simultaneously*):

On your way,
Make no stay;
Love lies awake,
Sleep rules a tyrant with a throne to shake,
With a sway to break.
So on your way,
On your way,
Make no stay.
Love lies awake,
Love you shall take –
And there's a power to break.
So take your way
And make no stay –
There's work to do today.
Have your way –
Smash that sway –

Break through his gates.
True love awaits.

HUGH *and* GEOFFREY *stride off towards the city. The lights dim out
and come up again on* REZIA *and* SELINA — *a sweet cuddlesome
blonde girl. They sit glumly on their campbeds.*

REZIA: You think they'll do it?

SELINA: They'll do it all right. There's been a lot of that
here lately. Stoning women.

REZIA: But that's for adultery – and we're not even married.

She is prepared to break down on that last word.

SELINA: Right. So they make out we're spies and we face
the firing squad.

REZIA: But that's only if there's a war on. Is there a war on?

SELINA: How would I know? No radio, no television, no
papers. There's another alternative I heard that fat one
talking about –

REZIA: In English?

SELINA: My Arabic's gotten to be pretty sound if they speak
slow enough. He spoke real slow, chewing the words like
he enjoyed them. They throw us in the street. Then the
students get us. They call them students but they don't
study anything. We're the enemy. Popular expression of
Islamic fervour and national loyalty. Tear the infidel to
shreds. The government does nothing. A good government really – still wants its money but it let the two
hostages go. Into the streets. Not the government's fault.
Their dirty hands are clean as clean.

REZIA: But surely our President will deliver the money
before then?

SELINA: Our President says no – a matter of principle.

REZIA: So we have to die on a matter of presidential
principle.

SELINA: And there's another alternative –

REZIA: How many alternatives are there?

SELINA: It's what they call a fate worse than death.

REZIA: There's no fate worse than death.

SELINA: Oh, I don't know. Having to accept the favours of that sex maniac that calls himself an ayatollah. And that's only holding off the final event. Have you smelt that man's halitosis?

REZIA: Oh, dear God.

They hear a horn in the distance.

SELINA: What's that – the mailman? Mr Pickwick? I must go to the bathroom and stand on the seat. You can see a lot from there.

She runs off. REZIA *winds her wristwatch and sings.*

No. 5 Finale

REZIA: What can I do? It's half past ten.
I watch the tread of empty time,
See one by one the minutes climb,
And then fall down and start again.

Once I read that time was not for lovers,
Lovers' clocks were heart and heart.
Now this sundered heart discovers
Time is wealth when lovers part.

Time's a wealth for lovers' spending,
But there is a limit set.
Time spins on but has an ending:
Time the thief will get us yet.

All I want is minutes only
Just to say: 'My heart, my own,
God, I've missed you, been so lonely' –
Then consent to die alone.

Can I mean those words sincerely?
No, my dearest love, I lie.
How can one who loves so dearly
Weakly yield – and meekly die?

SELINA *comes running back, breathless.*

SELINA:
Listen – hear – there's the buzzing of some special fuss.
Somebody's come – that means they've come for us.

REZIA:

Where? Who? Tell me – don't make me guess.

SELINA:

Two men have come and both in flying dress.
They've let them cross the frontier – and that means
one thing –
Ransom has arrived – our noble leader has said yes.
We're going to be freed, we're going home at last.
All our worries are past.

REZIA:

Oh, it's him! Yes, it's he!

BOTH:

Let it be true. After all this weary waiting,
Let it be true.
There's a martial ring thrilling the air,
There's a country's pride riding out there.
They will not bend the knee
But demand the freedom of two of their citizens,
daughters of the free.
Oh, make it true, oh make it truly true.
Let it be true. Let it be so. After all this endless
waiting
Smell in the air not despair – savour pride,
Rational passion of national pride.
Oh, make it true, truly true.
Often we've cried, often we've cried to be free.
Now let it be!

SELINA:

Hear? It's the guard. They're going to change the
guard,
To change it and double it, I hear.
You hear? The doubling of the guard.
There must be something that they fear.

REZIA:

And those higher voices? Eunuchs?

SELINA:

No, just tough kids.

THE GUARD (*off*):
>   Hear the final waktu's sigh,
>   Hear the bilal's yodelling cry
>   From his watchtower in the sky:
>   'No God but 'Allah, Allah most high.'
>   Now we have to go on guard
>   And patrol the palace yard.

REZIA (*simultaneously*):
>   Let my heart stop thudding hard
>   And my senses stand on guard.
>   Disappointment seeks my ear
>   And disillusion slithers near.
>   Let me soothe my throbbing head,
>   Put myself and it to bed.

The two girls prepare to undress, but a group of blackclad ladies comes in, accompanied by a couple of leering guards, with black glasses and guns. The girls shrug. SELINA *brings a pack of cards. The girls start to play on a soap box. The curtain falls and the act ends.*

ACT TWO

HUGH *and* GEOFFREY *sit, somewhat apprehensively, on the stage in front of the curtain. They have the magic horn, but nothing else.*

GEOFFREY: Well, we made it – so far.

HUGH: Magicked our way over the frontier. Magicked our way past the guards here. And then the magic stopped.

GEOFFREY: The horn's had its twenty-four hours off. It'll be ready to start again when we get in there. They were pretty good with us here, I guess. Knew we were something special.

HUGH: But we're locked in.

GEOFFREY: It's the kind of place where they lock people in. Especially the women.

HUGH: She'll be unlocked.

GEOFFREY: There are two of them.

HUGH: They'll both be unlocked. No shenanigins. Hand over the girls and we hand over the cash. Right?

GEOFFREY: But there's no cash.

HUGH: I give him this certified cheque. And while he's looking at it –

GEOFFREY: Tally ho. I hope he won't cash that – when we get out.

HUGH: The signature's a good forgery. It's been a long time, Geoff.

GEOFFREY: Her, you mean. Man, you've got problems. Now you've got to get married. End of the story.

HUGH: I want to.

GEOFFREY: Better you than me. You'll have to climb down

out of the deep blue heavens. Not that they *are* deep blue.
You know what women are like. When they get a man
they want him chained to something nice and safe. Not
test flying, oh no sir. And they want you all, boy. All of
you. Hurry home to the pot roast. I love my work. Ah,
no. Baby, you got to love me. No rivals.

HUGH: I know. That's what worries me.

The symphony to HUGH'*s aria begins.*

GEOFFREY: Dig that trumpet. Dig a hole for it first.

No. 6 Aria

HUGH:
>An airman's life is the only one,
>The moon's his friend, his lord's the sun.
>He's got stars to fleck the friendly sky
>And silver wings to lift him high,
>And silver wings to lift him high.
>Sure of my birdman's worth,
>Proud of my hawklike eye,
>Sure of my birdman's worth,
>Proud of my hawklike eye,
>I used to scorn the distant earth
>And only loved to fly – fly – fly – fly!

GEOFFREY: Aha – now the mood changes. Tune sounds
familiar. That's right. I heard it from the dressing room.

HUGH:
>But love calls me now
>To fold up my wings
>And learn to bend and bow
>My heart to love of earthier things.
>The bright evening hearth,
>The wife waiting there –
>The children climb my knees
>The envied kiss to share.

GEOFFREY: Gray's 'Elegy'.

HUGH:
>Fostering birth of love of the earth within me,
>Marital love, yes, marital love will win me –
>The walk with the twins lying snug in their carriage –

That will be marriage, marriage, marriage,
Marriage!

I love her, I love her, as no one can doubt.
Will this make my love of the air peter out?
But man's love must stand like a thing set apart;
We know it's woman's whole existence.

GEOFFREY: Byron.

HUGH:
So I must divide my heart
And resist woman's nature's insistance I give her all.
But I cannot give her all, not all,
I can't give her all.
My ear is inclined to another call.
Live without love?
I know no one who can.
But skill and adventure, daring and danger are part of
    a man.
Daring and danger – they're sewn underneath the
    skin of a man.
Skill and adventure, skill and danger –
These are a part of, a precious part of a man.
Skill and adventure, skill and danger –
These are a part of, a precious part of a man.
These are part of the bone and the being of a man.

GEOFFREY *claps, also, it is presumed, the audience. During the last orchestral measures, uniformed men indicate that* GEOFFREY *and* HUGH *follow them. They go off. The curtain rises on the court of the* AYATOLLAH HARUN. *A chorus sings his praises.*

No. 7 Chorus

Islam! Islam! Islam! Islam!
Oil and Allah build an unshakable tower.
Allah, shake the towers of the West and break their
    power.
Sickle moon and star beside it long proclaim our
    might.
Afrits and shaitans, kingdoms of the night
Now fall to dust, your engines turn to rust.
Long may our leader live to lead the kingdom of the
    just.

Allah!
Oil and Allah build an unshakable tower.
Allah, shake the towers of the West and break their
    power.
Sickle moon and star, may you scar the pagan night.
Allah and his prophet bring the world to the light.

Towards the end of this chorus, HUGH *and* GEOFFREY *are led on. They make rather American gestures to* HARUN *(whose full name is Harun ibn Abdul Rahab).* HARUN *is in Islamic robes with a round-loaf headdress. Prominent among his court is his brother,* LOT IBN ABDUL RAHAB. LOT *is conspicuous for his Western dress. He looks reliable.*

HUGH: Hugh MacLaren and –

GEOFFREY: Geoffrey Cabot –

HUGH: Special envoys from –

HARUN: I know what you are, I think. Your identifications were presumably established by the palace guard. You have the outstanding sum – thirty-three million dollars is the sum as it stands at present? I include, of course, the accumulated interest.

GEOFFREY: Sir, there is some dubiety about that interest.

HARUN: Not in my mind, nor in the minds of my financial advisers. I specified cash. You have not brought cash, I see. You have brought nothing apparently except that musical instrument.

HUGH: Cash was impossible. My country has rigorous regulations about the exportation of cash. I carry a certified cheque.

HARUN: Let me examine it.

HUGH: Let *me* examine the two hostages.

HARUN: Oh, very well. Let them be brought in.

No. 8

To the astonishment of HUGH *and* GEOFFREY, REZIA *and* SELINA *come in, dressed for leaving, carrying a bag each, in the midst of a group of Muslim girls in solemn black who execute minimal dance steps.*

HUGH (*rushing to her*):   Darling!

REZIA (*unable to get away from her surrounding escort*): Sweetheart!

SELINA (*to* GEOFFREY): Hi.

GEOFFREY (*to* SELINA): Well – hi.

HARUN: Arms longing to embrace held out – preparedness to kiss in public. Ugh. The decadent West. You need Islamic discipline.

GEOFFREY: We need Islamic oil.

HARUN: Eyes bulging with concupiscence. Lips dripping in lust. Lot, my brother, take away his horn.

HUGH: This horn stays with me. It's a gift from one even higher than the Ayatollah of Naraka, higher than the Queen of Great Britain and Northern Ireland, higher than the President of –

HARUN: Oh, you shall have it back when I've assured myself that it's not some new diabolic secret weapon. Poisoned darts fired by the pressure of its keys. A revival of the ancient blunderbuss with modern refinements. Take it, Lot.

Two attendants in black glasses with cocked pistols grab the horn and hand it to LOT, *who examines it with care.*

LOT: It seems to me to be an ordinary orchestral horn. Pitched in the key of F. I played one once in the college orchestra of Duke University.

HARUN: Yes, the Western education that ruined you. Decadent modern music. Train it on our Western visitors. Depress the keys. Blow it.

LOT: You don't actually *blow* a horn. You sort of spit into it and activate the air already there. Forgive me – playing it always used to give me a headache. If you'll permit me to plug my ears –

HARUN: Yes, a Western education made you weak in the head.

HUGH: Us too, sir. Do you mind if we don't listen? You too, girls, stick fingers in –

During the above lines LOT *takes a Kleenex packet from his pocket and sticks two wads in his ears. The girls and their rescuers stick in their fingers.*

LOT: Now – what shall it be? Ah yes – the opening bar of Weber's *Oberon*.

He intones the notes. At once the entire court is caught in a state of paralysis, except for the five of them.

LOT: Allah! It *is* a secret weapon. Allah Ta'alah. Good God. The higher harmonics working on the centres of muscular control. How long does the effect last?

HUGH: Long enough for you to effect a palace revolution. Down with tyranny. Long live a free Naraka friendly to the West. Kill him.

LOT: My own brother? Impossible.

GEOFFREY: Put him in the jug. Get on the state radio. Grab the army. Give us back that horn.

LOT: A new era commences, dedicated to individual freedom in all spheres – religious, political, sexual –

REZIA *has got over her astonishment at this miracle and now leaps into* HUGH's *arms. The two kiss passionately.* GEOFFREY *expects an amorous symmetry with* SELINA *but does not get it.*

GEOFFREY: We have to make our getaway. How?

LOT: This is the month of Ramadan and the airport doesn't function during the day. But my private helicopter's outside. Take it to the coast. There you can pick up some vessel or other. Go now. Long live liberty.

The five in unison sing the final phrase of No. 6 to the following words, then the four westerners get the hell out.

No. 6 *Tenth bar after Più allegro. Orchestra plays bar before it*

> Now let a period of total freedom commence –
> Based on love, toleration and decent common sense.

The curtain closes. Music from the Overture. Curtain rises to show our four Westerners at a port.

HUGH (*to* REZIA): Angelcake, you can tell me all about it when we get on board. The SS *Mohammed Ali* is moored round there. Let's see about getting tickets. You two stay here. We'll be back.

They go off, entwined. GEOFFREY *and* SELINA *look rather awkwardly at each other.*

GEOFFREY: Selina –

SELINA: Yes. That's my name.

GEOFFREY: A nice name too. Fitting, if you see what I mean.

SELINA: What *do you* mean?

GEOFFREY: It's got the right sounds – you have to smile when you say it. And a bit exotic – or is it erotic? I always get the two words mixed up. Listen, Selina –

SELINA: Are you proposing something?

GEOFFREY: Well, look at the circumstances. Those two always in each other's arms – and we – well, we ought to get better acquainted.

SELINA: How much better?

GEOFFREY: Do you find me repulsive?

SELINA: Not more than the average man.

GEOFFREY: You've had a bad time with average men, huh?

SELINA: With one. The one I was nearly married to. What *are* you proposing – marriage? So we can end up with a double wedding?

GEOFFREY: I've not had much experience with marriage. Well, that's an exaggeration. I've not had *any* experience. I've been around, of course. We could get married – after a bit. What they call a probationary period. Say yes.

SELINA: What to say yes?

GEOFFREY: To the probationary period.

SELINA: Listen, buster.

No. 9 *Arietta*

SELINA:

I loved a guy once before.
It was no great success.
So I must think some more
Before I answer no or yes.
This fellow became a bore.
He taught me cautiousness.
Love was not all it ought to be –
It disillusioned me.
I think a woman should be free –

Fancy free.
I see you don't agree,
So let us wait and see.

Just take my hand and learn
How to quench your impetuous fire,
And understand the fires that burn
In the hearth of a woman's desire.
A girl requires a certain tenderness,
A touch and not a clutch.
Your ardent ways don't please me much:
They're no royal road to success.
So let's try and cultivate a friendly rapport,
And if it leads to something more,
I'll be glad to accept your caress.
Not yet – not now.
I've got to teach you how
To know when I'm ready to say yes.

GEOFFREY *shrugs, grins ruefully and nods. Then he tries to take her in his arms.*

SELINA: Weren't listening, were you?

GEOFFREY: Well – that was just an aria. Sorry. It says arietta in the score. Please, Selina –

SELINA: Get away, you big ape.

HUGH *and* REZIA *rush in.*

HUGH: We've got tickets –

SELINA: How many berths?

HUGH: How many do you think? A coastal vessel. It takes us to Aden. There we pick up a plane for the good old – you know what. OK, Geoff?

GEOFFREY: Fine.

REZIA: I get seasick.

SELINA: Me too.

HUGH: We shan't be on the high seas. Hugging the coast. Hugging.

SELINA: Yeah, hugging.

No. 10 Quartet

HUGH AND GEOFFREY:
　Over the winedark way ahead,
　Over the foaming brew,
　There's a gay and glittering day ahead
　There – it awaits me and you, us two. So?

REZIA AND SELINA:
　Willingly I will embark on that ocean,
　Although I don't enjoy the ride.
　There's something in the thought of its motion
　Makes something turn, something churn in my inside.
　But we're ordained apparently cheerfully to go
　On the billowing boiling brine, so we dare not say no.

ALL:
　Aboard, then. Let's all get on board.
　Hear the engines throbbing low,
　Hear the engines throbbing low,
　The engines throbbing low.
　Upon the ocean's heaving breast
　We'll hope to get a little rest
　　{ And give intermitted love a chance to glow,
　　{ And give infant friendliness a chance to grow.
　So let's get aboard and enjoy the peace that life on a
　　ship can bring. Sing:
　Sailing is the only thing.
　There's something in its pitch and roll
　　{ Irradiates my very soul
　　{ That nauseates my very soul
　　{ But/And gives intermitted love a chance to glow
　　{ But/And gives infant friendliness a chance to grow.
　So let's get aboard and enjoy the peace that life on a
　　ship can bring. Sing:
　Sailing is the only thing.

*They go off towards the ship's siren, the men carrying the girls'
bags. The stage begins to darken. Faint distant lightning flashes.
Thunder distantly rumbles.* PUCK *comes in. He addresses the
audience.*

PUCK:　Well, they think it's all over. Little do they know,
　as they say. There are two distinct kinds of *they* there.

Never mind. Titania thinks that there's been no final proof as yet of eternal devotion. I work for her as well as Oberon, and there's a frequent collision of interests. Now we have to have a collision of natural forces. You'll see what I mean. You'll also hear me sing. You thought this was purely a speaking part? Little do you know, as they say.

No. 11 *Solo, chorus and storm*

PUCK:
Spirits of water, earth and air,
Spirits of fire, are you all there?
You who distract, disrupt, destroy,
I offer this proffer – a task you'll enjoy.
Quitting the caves where you love to lurk,
Come out of hiding and go to work.
Earth, sweet mother, shake your locks
And shake down volcanic rocks.
Water, healer of heat and thirst,
Do your curst worst, break and burst.
Winds children puff into toy balloons,
Be augmented into fierce typhoons.
Fire, bright companion of winter nights,
Be brilliant, be brilliant – your name's up in lights.

He indicates the lightning flash.

Obey my master's urgent call,
I mean Oberon, who rules us all.

ELEMENTS, *who appear in all parts of the stage, desperate monsters appropriately garbed*:
We are here, we are here.
Tell us what to do, tell us what to do.
Kick the moon in the rear?
Chop the sun into two?
Bring Apocalypse near,
Since it's well overdue?
Smash all nature and fashion its patterns anew?
Cook a Milky Way custard? A Zodiac stew?
Tell! Speak!
There's no end of things we can do.

PUCK: No, no – the only thing I ask
           Is quite an elementary task –
           A simple shipwreck on that shore.
           I'm sorry that it can't be more.

ELEMENTS: Wreck a ship?
           Just that? Just that? Just that?
           It's not worth the trip –
           You're losing your grip.
           You need us for killing a gnat?
           Playing patball?
           Top and whip?
           None the less,
           Our answer's yes.
           Click!
           It's on!
           We go, we go, we're gone!

The storm is unleashed. PUCK, *finding an umbrella to protect him,
gets off with difficulty. The storm rages in the orchestra, helped by
sound effects. On the cyclorama we see a labouring ship. The
curtain comes down. As the storm abates it comes up again.* HUGH
drags REZIA *out of the sea and lays her, unconscious and possibly
dead, on the sand. During the following preghiera he makes use of
pauses to give her artificial respiration.*

No. 12 *Preghiera*

HUGH: Mother taught me how to pray,
           But I threw the boon away.
           Save her, oh save her is what I should say,
           But who will hear – what *he* or *they*
           Will hover near
           To help? – or else to punish me,
           Yes, me, yes, me,
           For trusting in the sea?

           I beg that my plea
           (Bending my knee)
           Carry to the Maker of
           Earth, sky and sea –
           If such there be.
           Spare my love

    I humbly pray.
    That is all I have to say.

He resumes artificial respiration. REZIA *comes to.*

HUGH: Thank God, thank God. All my fault, dearest. I never really trusted ships. That's why I took to flying.

REZIA: It was terrible, terrible, Hugh. And I've lost all my things.

HUGH: We'll get you new ones in Aden. Damn, we've lost the horn.

REZIA: It wasn't much help, was it? When the storm started, I mean.

HUGH: It only works on things with brains. Or – if I blew it hard enough –

REZIA: You blew it hard enough. He didn't come.

HUGH: He probably couldn't hear, with all that racket.

REZIA: We seem to be the only ones saved. Where's Selina – where's Geoffrey?

HUGH: I saw them riding the waves on the door of the sauna room. They'll be all right. Are *you* all right, my angel?

REZIA: Cold. Hungry.

HUGH: I'll look inland. There must be some village or something. Jump up and down. Dry yourself. Sing.

REZIA: Sing? I haven't the energy.

HUGH: I'll be as quick as I can. I'll try and keep within earshot. If you're singing I'll know all's well. So long, my love.

He kisses her and goes off. REZIA *is left alone.*

REZIA: Sing, he says. What was that song I used to sing in the Western Amateur Opera Company in Naraka? Not really a song. But it's appropriate.

No. 13 *Scene and aria*

REZIA:
    Ocean, you mighty monster,
    You are curled
    Like some green snake
    Around the living world.
    Dangerous enough when resting from the gale,

A playground for the dolphin and the whale.
But when you rear and hiss and strike as now,
And gnaw the labouring ship from stern to bow,
Chewing the mainmast and the garboard strake,
Then, dragon sea, like you we cry and quake.
Green and black, snowy, lacy-fleeced,
Heaves in arms the heavy beast,
Grendel seeks his fleshly feast.
Shoreside bell, knell. Dear ones, weep now.
Ocean's victims greenly sleep now.

But see – I see the sea grow calmer –
Hangman loosening the noose,
Soldier taking off his armour.
He declares, though grudgingly, a truce.
Let the beating pulse grow limper,
Let the clouds dissolve to fog,
And the gale become a whimper,
As of a fireside-dreaming dog.

The sun breaks weak but warm,
The sea's a jeweller's shop.
Like time itself, each storm
Must have a stop.

Sunset melts the cloudy webbing,
And the breezes moan in pity
As I see the lifeblood ebbing
From a bombed and blazing city.

This may be the last occasion
I shall be the witness of
Sea and sun and joy's invasion
At all blessings from above,
And be blessed with faultless love.

But there's something on the sea,
Something cream-and-silver-shining.
It's a dolphin or, maybe,
Killer shark that's finished dining.

No, I see it now – a boat!
Yes – new-rinsed and bright – a sail.
Whose buoyant skill has kept afloat
Such a prey to the gale?

We're safe at last.
Oh, Hugh, where are you?
All our troubles are done, all buried in the past.
Make haste, gallant mast,
To us who were cast
On a friendless coast without a hope in view!

Quick – quick – give a sign now –
This scarf, this foulard, will do fine now.
They've seen me and answer this signal of mine.
Hurry, hurry, Hugh love.
Run now, run now, run now, run now,
Hugh, my love!

With the gliding of a dancer
On the floor of a ballroom.
It is riding like a lancer,
Though this shore gives them small room
For their lay to.
They too smile!
Dearest, we will be home in a while.

With the gliding of a dancer
On the floor of a ballroom
It is riding like a lancer
With the answer
To all the rumours whispered by despair
That made us share a living hell.
All is well –
I can tell.

All is not well. HARUN, *the deposed ayatollah, comes ashore, in smart decadent Western sea clothes, accompanied by a gang of armed thugs.* REZIA *tries to run, but they grab her.*

HARUN: Where is he?

REZIA: Dead, dead, all dead. Let me go.

HARUN: I'm sure you'd like to be with your companions. That can be arranged, but it will be a slower business than a mere storm at sea. You fooled me, you all did. I demand justice. The West doesn't always pay its debts. But I never fail to pay mine.

REZIA: What are you going to do to me?

HARUN: Take you to my istana on this quite populous

island. An alternative capital to the state of which I am
still the lawful ruler. My brother's a fool. Stone dead hath
no fellow. That ought to be from the Koran, but it was
said by some decadent Western ruler. What you should
say now is: how do you propose to get back to power?
Go on, say it.

REZIA: Let me go. I've done no harm. I've never been inter-
ested in politics.

HARUN: Those are the ones who suffer. On my island here
I have a nuclear rocket aimed at the heart of Naraka.
My brother will scuttle away to Cannes or Cap d'Ail or
somewhere, and things will be as they were before. But
first – a man is entitled to a little pleasure, especially when
he's suffered. It was quite a job getting that jail blown up.
Come on.

They drag REZIA *away, crying Hugh's name.*

No. 13a

This music covers the entrance of SELINA *and* GEOFFREY. *They are
drying in the sun but are terribly bedraggled.* SELINA *clutches her
suitcase. They sit down wearily.*

SELINA: This is no better than the other place.

GEOFFREY: No worse either.

SELINA: What are we going to do?

GEOFFREY: Get dry. Warm up a little. Then sleep.

SELINA: How warm up a little?

GEOFFREY: There's only one way that suggests itself.

SELINA: How did you know I'd got a brandy flask in this
bag?

GEOFFREY: Brandy? Open up, quick. Anything to eat?

SELINA (*opening up*):   Only these peanuts in their waterproof
wrapping. Oh God, everything's soaked.

GEOFFREY: It'll all dry.

He drinks from the flask and gobbles peanuts.

SELINA: Do you think they're – you know – alive?

GEOFFREY: *We* are, baby.

SELINA: That's selfish.

GEOFFREY: You want us to have died with them?

SELINA: I guess not. (*A pause.*) What do you propose? I mean, when we get back – if we get back –

GEOFFREY: We've been through too much together just to – well – split. We kind of belong to each other.

SELINA: And where will we belong to each other?

GEOFFREY: Boston. Massachusetts.

SELINA: I know where Boston is, stupid. Where they eat baked beans and boiled scrod.

GEOFFREY: We have it broiled sometimes. Where are you from?

SELINA: Albuquerque. New Mexico.

GEOFFREY: I know where Albuquerque is. Stupid.

SELINA: Don't call me stupid, stupid.

GEOFFREY: Darling, then. Honey. Light of my life. I know a lot of love poetry too. I wanted to be a poet once. Before I took to the air.

SELINA: So I'll be putting the beans into the pot and look up at you waving down.

GEOFFREY: I don't like beans all that much.

SELINA: I could eat some now. And some scrod.

GEOFFREY: Broiled for preference. With Boston cream pie afterwards.

SELINA: That's fattening.

GEOFFREY: I'll love you even when you're fat. Honey. My fat little honeypot. Come on. Let's make blankets of each other and hit the sack. I'm bushed.

SELINA: Yeah, bushed. Geoff –

GEOFFREY: Yes?

SELINA: What or who is this Oberon guy? I thought he was just someone in Shakespeare – you know, that play with Bottom in it. And you say you've met him. Were you stoned?

GEOFFREY: I met him all right. He used to be called the fairy king. I always liked the idea of fairies – you know, real ones – not fags, like those down there in the orchestra.

SELINA: How do you know there are fags down there?

GEOFFREY: It says so in the score. Fag One and Fag Two.

SELINA: You dope. Fag means fagotto. A fagotto's a bassoon.

GEOFFREY: You're right. I forgotto.

SELINA: You're terrible. Sleep.

GEOFFREY: Yeah. To a fairy song. Philomel with melody – sing in our sweet lullaby – lullaby –

SELINA: That's Mendelssohn. We've got to stick to Weber. That's laid down.

GEOFFREY (*dropping off*):   Or mermaids. I kind of like the idea of mermaids. A goodnight kiss?

They exchange one and then start to sleep in each other's arms. OBERON *and* PUCK *appear.*

PUCK: Poor earth children.

OBERON: Sleep spirits, lie heavy on their eyelids. Let's have some sleep-inducing music.

PUCK: Why not mermaids?

OBERON: Why not?

It is now dark, but there is a phosphorescence on the sea on the cyclorama. A MERMAID *appears and sings. There will be another later.*

No. 14 Finale

MERMAID I:
　　Life is good in my watery bed
　　Where I brood on life in the world overhead.
　　How do they breathe in that razorsharp air?
　　What do they eat? There's no plankton floating up
　　　　there.
　　Sometimes I soar to the roof of our world,
　　Head under that water that's mother-of-pearled.
　　Pearl up there, are you king of the sky?
　　Where is the shell of the oyster that taught you to fly?

The moon bathes the scene opalescently. Another MERMAID *appears and sings.*

MERMAID 2:
>Now and then I can see up aloft
>A small flying fish with a buzzing so soft
>The stars in their meadow, ignoring its flight,
>Find themselves swallowed in mouthfuls of light.
>But when the day's octopus blazes with red,
>I plunge to the depths and go sweetly to bed.
>Cods and scrods, all alive alive oh –
>Life's dripping wet in the watery waters below.

PUCK:
>Master – see – that male one there –
>He believes in fairies, yes?
>He deserves a fairy dream
>Before he wakes to new distress.

OBERON:
>Chorus by a fairy crew.
>Chorus master – me or you?

BOTH:
>Fairies, goblins, dapper elves,
>Join in with the sea nymphs and try to sing
>>yourselves.
>Let all those fishy folk wake from their trance
>And discover that you too can sing and dance:
>Make it midsummer night tonight
>And blow on the glowworms to give more light
>And clean up your wings so they'll give you a
>>smoother flight.
>Fairies, goblins –
>Though you are only a dream,
>Let it seem that you're real tonight.

MERMAIDS:
>Since you earthfolk seem to need our song,
>We will join the dream and play along.

FAIRIES, ETC.:
>We do not get out all that much,
>Dancing, flirting, warbling and such,
>But the moon calls all of us to play,

White noises fall from the Milky Way.
Merrily merrily let us play,
Merrily merrily let us try
A circuitous way
Over the sea
Or the starlit sky.
{ Swimming for me –
{ Sea's not for me –
{ They prefer to fly.
{ I prefer to fly.

Elvish horns – tarara –
Groanings from old Triton's conch –
Hear those horns – tarara –
Mingle with the bullfrog's honk.
Let us sing merrily, merrily let us sing.

The chorus continues till the moon starts to fade. The sleeping lovers continue to sleep, locked in each other's arms. The orchestra quietly brings the act to an end.

ACT THREE

Brief Prelude: perhaps the opening of the Overture. The scene is still the seashore – gulls, breeze, the hissing of the shingle, the plaint of the waves. The two new lovers sleep. But SELINA *suddenly wakes. She looks at* GEOFFREY, *who comfortably snores. She feels a little chilly.*

SELINA: I was dreaming about being warm. I was dreaming about being home. Ah well, I'm neither. But I can still dream, even when I'm awake. (*She yawns.*) Just about awake.

No. 15 Aria

SELINA:
New Mexico,
New Mexico;
The state where I was born.
Where Pluto's palace broods below
The miles of waving corn.
I dreamed I was in Santa Fé,
Back at the old State U.
Where I strove so hard to achieve an A
But had some good times too.
I'd visit the pueblos just to hear
The Mexican guitars,
Or eat my tacos and sip my beer
Under Albuquerque's stars.

Olé olé olé –
Oh the times that I knew.
Olé olé olé –
With the sun crashing down from a merciless blue.
Back in old Albuquerque

And old Santa Fé,
And one day in Roswell
I fell, like a bale of hay.
Olé olé olé –
Oh, my first steady one,
And the things that we did in the heat of the sun.
Though I should wish him dead,
It is easier said than done.
Olé olé olé!

Olé olé olé –
I must start out anew.
Olé olé olé –
And I'll try pretty hard to make something of you.
So goodbye, Albuquerque,
So long, Santa Fé.
It looks like New England's the place where I have to
    stay.
Olé olé olé –
That's the call of the wild.
But it's time to be tamed and get sorted and filed
– A respectable bed
In the ranks of the wed, my child.

Olé olé olé!

GEOFFREY (*waking blearily*): I dreamed you were singing about New Mexico. But before that I dreamed about fairies. And in the middle I dreamed – ah, never mind. I can't bear to recall it.

SELINA: Recall it. So long as it wasn't about food.

GEOFFREY: It was. In a way. No, all the way. No, not all the way.

SELINA: Make up your mind, brother.

No. 17 Duet

GEOFFREY:
    I was dreaming that my breakfast was laid
    In the glow of summer Sunday –
    Bacon and eggs and toast and marmalade,
    And the evil thought of Monday
    Told to go and loop the loop.

Coffee perking gaily
And the Sunday paper on the stoop,
Full of laughs and full of poop,
And so much bigger than the daily.
Nothing's better, I would say,
Than a godless Sabbath day.

SELINA:

When we two are made one flesh –
Though you're tanned and I am pearly –
You will get your coffee fresh,
But you'll get it good and early.
Smart as paint we'll amble off
To a show of Christian piety,
Where assembled worshippers will cough
At the sermon's grim sobriety.
Then I'll get the oven hot
For whatever Sunday joint we've got
And potatoes in the pot.

GEOFFREY:

Will it really be such heaven?

SELINA:

Sunday service at eleven. Then a free day. Why not?

GEOFFREY:

A crazy dream. Yeah, we're free – apparently to die
here.

BOTH:

Let's keep dreaming – of a future.
Sunday morning, Saturday night –
Drinking, dancing – then just the pair of us.
Saturday evening – isn't that right?
So let the gods of gloom beware of us.
Loving our laughter
And everything after,
With just us two a-raising the rafter.
Raising sweet hell in some bar,
So they'll know the kind we are,
Drinking, laughing, joking, shoving,
Finally loving,
Loving loving loving loving!

HUGH *comes in, torn, bleeding, depressed. He sees the two with qualified joy. He carries a bag.*

HUGH: Thank God, thank God, thank God – but where is she?

GEOFFREY: Rezia's alive?

HUGH: I left her here. Fit, well, lovely, safe. While I went foraging.

GEOFFREY: How long ago?

HUGH: Yesterday. Before sunset. I went looking for food. Are you hungry?

SELINA: What kind of thing *is* food? Give me that.

She and GEOFFREY *tear open the sack, finding bread, something suspiciously like ham (if this is Muslim territory) and a bottle of something, probably* haram *wine.*

HUGH: Then I got captured.

GEOFFREY (*mouth full*): Baptureb?

HUGH: There were these like bandits. They could see I was white so they thought I was rich. Then they saw I had nothing except my watch. And a few dollars. Then they started to talk about ransoms. Then I got mad. Then they got convinced there was nothing in me for them. Then they told me Harun was here.

SELINA: Here? He's in jail.

HUGH: No. He's here, they said. They saw his boat come. He's got some kind of atomic installation here, they said. I didn't believe that. Then I thought – why not? He's a cunning bastard. What's this? (*He picks up a scarf, the one* REZIA *used as a distress signal.*) God, it's hers. Footprints. Did you see those before?

SELINA: We were too bushed to start looking for footprints.

GEOFFREY: And it was too dark.

HUGH: I see it now. They landed here. They got her. And I'm going to get her.

No. 16 Terzettino

HUGH:
I'm going now to find her.

GEOFFREY:
   You don't know where she is.

HUGH:
   I'll tear the bonds that bind her.
   Tigers would be kinder
   To him I'm going to grind
   Till they won't know that his face is his.

SELINA:
   God go with you, but go disguised.
   I've got a costume to take home as a present.
   Just put these things on: be a female peasant,
   Coming for a job that was advertised.

HUGH:
   I'll find out the place and get in somehow.

SELINA:
   You can get in somehow.

GEOFFREY:
   Get there somehow.

HUGH:
   So I'd better get on with it now.

SELINA:
   Start your rescue now.

GEOFFREY:
   Get off now.

TOGETHER:
   Armed with a broom
   For sweeping the yard,
   Creep past the room where they house the guard.
   Let them be kissed
   With your/my good strong fist.
   They won't resist.

HUGH:
   This is far too optimistic – but still I'll try.

SELINA:
   This may seem a too optimistic dream, but have a try.

GEOFFREY:
   Let's be optimistic, for at least you can try.

TOGETHER:
    Up with your/my fist –
    Or you've/I've kissed her goodbye.

HUGH: I can't do it – I know I can't. They search everybody – they're bound to. If only we had the horn.

GEOFFREY: Slipped overboard. A squid's home now.

HUGH: But he's bound to help, isn't he? He knows what's going on. It's in his interest to help – proof of eternal love and so on.

SELINA: What *is* this?

GEOFFREY: A long story for the winter's fire. Back in Boston. Not now.

HUGH: I have to trust. I've got to have faith. There *has* to be a happy ending.

GEOFFREY: It's that sort of opera, I think. It's also called *Oberon*. That means he has to come in at the end.

HUGH: To recite an elegy for dead lovers.

GEOFFREY: No. I'm pretty sure this isn't a tragedy.

HUGH: My poor love. Poor girl. I wonder what he's doing to her.

The stage grows dark except for a patch of light which shows the imprisoned REZIA. *She sings.*

No. 18 Cavatina

REZIA: One escape, why not two?
    Who would come to my shout?
    Nobody but a crew
    That's been trained to look out.

    Held in the clutch of a strong evil man –
    I can't escape. I'm helpless –
    But I'll clutch what hope I can.

    If this were an opera
    I'd find it absurd –
    Such a gross piece of crude melodrama –
    Crude is the word.

    That ought to make it easy
    To accept the foully obscene –

Things that I've merely read about
In some bestseller or cheap magazine.

The trembling violins
Will sound their alarms.
My hero is coming –
I'll melt in his arms.

That event is not going to happen,
And the 'cellos agree.
But I can't believe
This is happening to me.

Fiction's heroines never fail
To make their getaway.
But this is no tale.
This is not a play.

She buries her head in her hands, distraught. Her image fades. We are back on the shore. HUGH *has changed into his female Arab costume, complete with yashmak – not, at the moment, in place.*

HUGH: I have to hope. And I'd better hope in him. What they call the god from the machine.

SELINA: Yeah – *deus ex machina*. We had that in a drama course at the U. Meantime, take some hope out of this.

She hands him the brandy flask. He sips then glugs from it.

GEOFFREY: That's the boy. Better?

HUGH: Wow. I'll win. I'm off. But I'd better sing first, hadn't I?

GEOFFREY: That's what you're here for.

No. 18a Rondo

HUGH:

I'm flying in hope and love and pain.
A fire burns fiercely inside my brain.
Heart, keep on pounding like countless drums.
Hear, my lover – your lover comes.

I feel like the Hudson new-unlocked
From the winter ice that kept it blocked,
Racing under Manhattan's heights,
Splitting the sun in refracted lights.

I'm flying in hope and love and fear,
The fear that love's implanted here.
All love gives is a golden cross –
We love the gold, we foresee its loss.

I'm flying in hope and love and pain.
A trumpet's shrilling inside my brain.
Hear my arterial kettledrums.
Hear, my love – your lover comes.

On that, he goes boldly off, his yashmak in position. GEOFFREY
and SELINA *look at each other.*

SELINA: Oughtn't we to follow him?

GEOFFREY: And get chopped ourselves?

SELINA: Will *he* get chopped?

GEOFFREY: That's not the point. He's got to do it. I mean,
I'd do it if you –

SELINA: But I'm not.

GEOFFREY: Not what?

SELINA: In her position. Do you see what I see?

She looks to the shore. So does he.

GEOFFREY: I don't believe it. Metal sinks.

SELINA: Not if it's stuck on a bit of plank.

GEOFFREY (*coaxingly*):   Come on, boy, good boy, come on.

SELINA: You scared of getting your tootsies wet?

GEOFFREY: No need. It's coming right in.

SELINA: So what do we do with it?

GEOFFREY: Can't you guess?

*The curtain closes. No. 19 starts on the orchestra. The curtain rises
to show a harem of seductive females, clad minimally. As someone
will say later,* HARUN *is a hypocrite.*

No. 19 *Chorus, solo and ballet*

GIRLS: Beguilers of leisure,
The toys of a Musulman's paradise,
Mere engines of pleasure,
Where pleasure has no price.

Reluctant houris,
Less than divine –
All our seductive allure is
Cast like pearls before swine.

HUGH *comes in. He keeps his yashmak on but his voice gives him away.*

HUGH: Where can I find – ?

GIRLS: It's a man – how did he get in?

HUGH (*singing*):
Quiet! Quiet!
Women have a right of choice.
I feel the same as you.
I don't hold the Muslim view.
Call me Liberation's voice.
I will rescue you from here
When I liberate my dear.

GIRLS:
You mean the hostage from the West –
She who taught us to protest?
She is under lock and key,
A voice of the free that's far from free.
She'll be here, no doubt at all,
When our lord and master comes to call.

HUGH:
You must be wondering just what I'll do
When this man we detest heaves into view.
Well, to be honest, I'm wondering too,
But I've more cause to cultivate hope than you.
You won't have heard
Of a certain power
Who gave his word at the opportune hour
Firmly to flame
All that power on.
Do you know his name?
Well, it's Oberon.

ONE OF THE GIRLS: He's coming now. Hide behind us.

HUGH *does so.* HARUN, *with the captive* REZIA *and all his personal bodyguard, comes in. He sits down. Whisky and cigars are brought.*

HARUN: Go on, sing.

GIRLS: The Prophet Mohammed
                Has promised his sons
                A green-growing garden
                Where cool water runs –

                A fleshly reward
                For the spirits of the just –
                A sanctification of appetite,
                A hallowing of lust.

                But you, Ayatollah,
                The scintillant light of Islam,
                Enjoy present paradise
                Where nothing is *haram*.
                You eat sausage-meat canapés,
                And cognac-flavoured jam.

                It's heaven, very very heaven,
                Very very heaven
                For the scintillant light of Islam.

                Your houris here assembled,
                As you know, have trembled
                With anticipation
                At the whetting of your desire –
                As the kindling and the paper
                And the wood await the taper
                That will set the hearth on fire.

HARUN: Dance! Stop now. Listen, all of you. There have
been false rumours going around. The end of Harun and
the start of the reign of Lot his brother. The beginning of
what the decadent West calls a freer life. Know, then, that
Harun is very firmly set on his throne. Lot is under arrest.
The strict rule of Islam continues. The West will soon
begin to tremble at the power of Naraka. Tonight we
express our contempt for the West through the due
execution of one of its daughters. Execution in the good
old Islamic way – as decreed by the Koran. The knife. The
axe. The mandatory torture of the infidel offender. Bring
her to me. (*But the girls surround her.* HARUN *comes forward,
incredulous.*) You dare? Womanly solidarity? Bring the
whip, Ahmad. (AHMAD, *a tough tall thug, brings the whip.*)

Start, Ahmad. A seraglio must learn that it is only an expendable parcel of nugatory sweets.

As AHMAD *raises the whip,* HUGH *grasps it. He pulls down his hood and yashmak.* REZIA *runs to him.*

REZIA: Oh God, oh God, you're here. At least we can –

HARUN: – Die together. You've been reading too many decadent Western shopgirl romances. Well, sir, congratulations. May I ask how you managed to join my houris?

HUGH: Your guards are no good. If I were you, I'd fire the lot of them.

HARUN: Get that whip off him. (*The whip is wrested from him, with a struggle.* HARUN *draws a revolver.*) I think the sooner these two are out of the way the better. Get out, houris. I hate the noise of female wailing. (*The girls are roughly thrust out of the room.*) Say your Christian prayers.

He levels the gun. The voice of GEOFFREY *is heard outside.*

GEOFFREY (*off*): Hugh! Ears!

HUGH *and* REZIA *know exactly what he means. They cover their ears. The horn blows without. Immediate paralysis for* HARUN *and his entourage. But* GEOFFREY *and* SELINA *are brought in in the grasp of two tough men of repulsive appearance.*

GEOFFREY: These two are deaf.

ONE OF THEM: *He's* deaf, not I. I'm merely insensitive to the effect on the nervous system of the higher harmonics. See.

He carries the horn. He raises to his lips the magical shining instrument. The rest wonder what is going to happen. As soon as he blows, the thing starts playing a dance tune of its own accord. He drops the horn, scared. GEOFFREY *picks it up. It goes on playing. The effect of the music is to make the formerly paralysed now dance.*

No. 20 Finale

The dancing men sing.

MALE VOICES:
> Hear! Music is playing!
> Hear! Such delicious noise.
> Hear! Shake a foot,
> Start dancing, you boys.

What's the music saying?
It's telling us to prance, dance, dance!

REZIA, SELINA, GEOFFREY, HUGH:
  At last! At last! All our trials are finished,
  Diminished their power, our enemies dance.
  They throw down their rifles,
  They'd throw down their knives.
  If their wives were here,
  They would dance with their wives.

During the above, LOT *comes in with an armed guard. He smiles at his Western friends, then he speaks over the music.*

LOT: This time, no leniency. I think it's his hypocrisy more than his villainy that makes me so sick. Whisky. The pleasures of the senses. Ugh. Tell your President to expect a confirmation of the oil deal. At favourable rates. Come, dance them off.

His captives dance off.

REZIA, SELINA, GEOFFREY, HUGH:
  Enough is enough, though.
  Time moves on.
  A single last blast should bring
  Oberon.

And so it does. GEOFFREY *blasts loudly.* OBERON *and* TITANIA *appear, above. They embrace lovingly.* PUCK *is with them.*

OBERON:
  Proved are your powers of tough endurance.
  Titania needs no more assurance
  That faithful love exists in men –
  In women too. The world is safe again.

  Now, by the way you came,
  By teletransportation,
  In the capital city of your nation
  Alight as flint lights flame.

  Tell your country's cream
  That a tyrant's dead and gone.
  Fuelled by a friendly and oil-rich regime,
  May your dream carry on.
  But let injustice and chicanery
  Beware of Oberon.

We will be embarking soon
On a second loving honeymoon.
Mother Nature heaves a grateful sigh.
Grateful am I.
Now – goodbye.

He, TITANIA and PUCK leave. The stage darkens. The four West-erners are whisked off. At the back of the stage a curious national flag descends – big stars and a wavy set of stripes. To martial music distinguished ladies and gentlemen come in. The lights come up. Finally we see the President. Then our four are led in. HUGH bows and speaks, sings rather.

HUGH: Dispatched by motives of the purest love
To release this lovely captive one,
I found a hawk's egg hatching in the covert of the
dove.
And so a deed was done
I had not expected to do.
A little war was won,
A victory for you,
O red, O white, O blue!

Bells ring in the key of D major. During the final chorus the President presents medals to the four.

CHORUS: Hats off to freedom and all who strive
To keep tyranny under and freedom alive.
God will preserve our historic right
To fight any bastard we wish to fight.
May God bless our boys with that light in their eyes
Which drives them to gain the ineffable prize.
May God bless our women, whose beauty is such
That no man who dies for it dies too much.
May God bless our Hugh
And Rezia too
And you two whose names we cannot recall,
And God bless us all,
And may God bless you.

TITANIA and OBERON are seen high above the patriotic flag, locked in a loving embrace. PUCK leaps down from their plinth, performs cartwheels and frightens the ladies. The curtain falls.

OBERON

A Romantic and Fairy Opera

IN THREE ACTS

by J. R. Planché

AS PERFORMED WITH THE MUSIC OF
The Baron Carl Maria von Weber

CHARACTERS

Charlemagne, Emperor of the Franks
Sir Huon of Bourdeaux, Duke of Guienne
Sherasmin, his Squire
Harouin Alraschid, Caliph
Babekan, a Saracen Prince
Almanzor, Emir of Tunis
First Saracen
Second Saracen
Third Saracen
Fourth Saracen
Abdallah (a Corsair)
Oberon, King of the Fairies
Puck
Fairy
Negro Slave
Captain of a Vessel
Sea Nymph
Titania
Two Cupids

Reiza, Daughter of Haroun
Fatima, her Attendant
Rashana, Wife of Almanzor
Namouna, Fatima's Grandmother
Nadina, a female of Almanzor's haram

ACT I

Scene I

OBERON'*s bower. At the rising of the curtain, several picturesque groups of Fairies are discovered, who sing the following*

CHORUS (*pianissimo*):

> Light as fairy foot can fall,
> Pace, ye Elves, your master's hall;
> All too loud the fountains play,
>   All too loud the zephyrs sigh;
> Chase the noisy gnat away,
>   Keep the bee from humming by
> Stretch'd upon his lily bed,
>   Oberon in slumber lies;
> Sleep, at length, her balm hath shed
>   O'er his long-unclosed eyes.
> O, may her spell as kindly bring
> Peace to the heart of the fairy king!

During the chorus, other FAIRIES *and* SPIRITS *enter and dance.*

Enter PUCK.

PUCK: How now? How now? Why do you loiter here?
     Are there not tasks to do? The sinking sun
     Is not an hour's journey from the sea,
     And you will deem it hard, I warrant me,
     When winking stars proclaim the time for sport,
     To be denied the dance. Should Oberon –

FAIRY: We did but watch, that nothing might disturb
     Our master's slumber.

PUCK: Dost thou prate, vile scum?
     Skip hence! or by the seal of Solomon –

                         (*Exeunt* FAIRIES.)

     He sleeps then still. 'Tis the first time his lids
     Have closed since he and fair Titania parted.
     Mere wife and husband could not well have wrangled

On slighter grounds, – which was most inconstant,
Woman or man? Ha! ha! The queen of course
Champion'd her sex, – debates rose high, – in anger,
One east, one west, – they speeded as of yore,
Swearing by all that fairies reverence,
Never to meet in love, till some fond pair,
Through weal and woe, 'mid flood, and chains, and fire,
Should keep their plighted faith inviolate,
Unmoved by pleasure, and unbent by pain!
And now the moody king would give his crown
To find this pair of turtles, and redeem
His hasty pledge. And, – for he knows 'tis vain
To trust to chance, – he spares nor sprite nor spell
To bring about the miracle. But hold, –
He wakes! He moves this way: I will retire
And mark his mood, ere I do speak with him.

Enter OBERON.

SONG

OBERON:
  Fatal oath! not even slumber
   Can thy victim's torture tame!
  Of my woes it swells the number,
   Of my wrath it feeds the flame.

  Still I burn, and still I languish,
   Doubled in my dream I feel
  All my age, and all my anguish;
   But no balm their wounds to heal.

PUCK (*advancing*):
  Hail, master!

OBERON:
  Tardy Spirit, is it thou?
  Where hast thou been since cock-crow?

PUCK: Round the globe;
  Through India and Cathay, across the sea
  Which rolls between them and that western world
  Unknown as yet to Frank or Saracen;
  Touched at each isle that studs the southern wave;
  On his own sands outraced the dromedary;
  Pass'd the strong-pinioned eagle in his flight
  O'er busy Europe; glanced like summer-light'ning
  From pole to pole – in hopes of finding that
  Which might console my king.

OBERON:
  My faithful Puck!
  How could I doubt thy zeal? Speak on, true servant!

PUCK: Alack! I cannot speak what thou wouldst hear.
Faith I have found, which peril could not shake,
Love I have seen, which absence could not cool,
Passion, which triumph'd over mortal pain;
But none that spotless pass'd the harder trial
Of proud prosperity! Nay, good my master,
Droop not: – Come, come, I have a tale for thee,
Will wake thy wonder.

OBERON:
Thou dost wake it now:
For where's the thing shall make the elf-king wonder,
Save *that* thou'st sought in vain, a constant woman?

PUCK: Some two hours since I stood beside the throne
Of Charlemagne, and heard the strangest sentence
Pass'd on a Paladin, that ever tongue
Of wrathful monarch spake. His son, Prince Scharlot,
Waylaid the young Sir Huon of Bourdeaux,
And foully would have slain him; but, defeated
In the attempt, paid with his own vile life,
In open fight, the forfeit of his treason.
France with one voice declared Sir Huon guiltless:
Noble and knight around the monarch kneeling
Sued for his grace; but o'er the juster king
The partial father triumphed, – 'Hence!' he cried:
'Thou hast thy life, but mark on what conditions!
Speed thee to Bagdad: seek the caliph's hall;
And there on some high festival, before
The assembled court, e'en at the banquet board,
Slay him who sits upon Haroun's left hand;
Then kiss, and claim his daughter as thy bride!'

OBERON:
And rides he forth upon this perilous quest?

PUCK: Ay, master.

OBERON:
And alone?

PUCK: A single squire,
A foolish, faithful varlet, follows him.

OBERON:
Hie thee back, Spirit, over land and sea,
Swifter than thought, till thou dost meet with them;
Cast a deep sleep on both, and bring them hither
Before the breath be cold that bids thee.

                              (PUCK *vanishes.*)

Yes!
The fairy king Sir Huon shall befriend,
And the true knight in turn his woes may end.

The stage opens, and a flowery bank rises, on which SIR HUON *and* SHERASMIN *are seen asleep;* PUCK *standing beside them.*

PUCK (*runs to* OBERON):
>   King of fairy land, 'tis done;
>   Knight and 'squire thou lookest on.

OBERON: That's my good goblin! (*Observing* SIR HUON.)

SONG

>   Ha! by starry night!
>   In this mailed breast, I ween,
>   Love a guest hath never been!
>   But my piercing eye can see,
>   Should he once installed be,
>   Pleasure, peril, pomp, or pain,
>   Him to shake may strive in vain!
>   Quickly to his charmed eyes
>   Let a pleasing vision rise   *Clouds envelope*
>   Of the caliph's lovely child   *the stage*
>   Whom now he seeks on errand wild,
>   And within the same short hour,
>   In far Bagdad's haram bow'r,
>   To the sleeping lady's sight
>   Shall the image of the knight
>   Be shown, and equal love impart,
>   Linking firmly heart to heart
>   Spirits, hear your master's spell:
>   Up! and do my bidding well.

(Music.)

The clouds open, and discover the interior of a Persian kiosk. REIZA *is seen seated on a couch in a melancholy attitude, with a lute in her hand. She rises and sings.*

SONG

>   O, why art thou sleeping, Sir Huon the brave?
>   A maiden is weeping by Babylon's wave.
>   Up, up, gallant knight, ere a victim she falls.
>   Guienne to the rescue! 'tis beauty that calls.

The vision disappears; clouds again enclose the kiosk, and then draw off to the Fairies' hall, as at first.

OBERON: Enough! Enough! the spell I break,
>   Children of the Earth, awake!

SHERASMIN (*waking*):
>   Eh! Oh! O dear! Sir! Master!

(Shakes SIR HUON.)

SIR HUON (*waking*):
    Stay, loveliest! For pity's sake!
    Gone! – Where am I? Ha! (*Seeing* OBERON.)

OBERON:
    Fear not, Sir Huon of Bourdeaux! Thou seest
    A friend who knows thee and thine errand. I
    Am Oberon, the king of fairy land.

SHERASMIN (*still more frightened*):
    Fairy! O! O! O! O!

OBERON:
    Peace, varlet! Hear me, Paladin.
    Relentless Charlemagne would have thy blood;
    But thou shalt execute his dread command,
    And to thy native France triumphantly
    Bear back thy beauteous bride, rest thou but true
    Amidst the trials fate prepares for thee.
    Therefore receive, Sir Duke, this iv'ry horn;
    Whatever danger may thy path beset,
    Its slightest sound will bring me sudden aid;
    Need'st thou the presence of the fairy king,
    A bolder blast will bring me to thy side,
    Tho' planets roll'd between us.   (*Brings the cup.*)
    Now to thee,
    Friend Sherasmin, I turn. Approach – nay, nearer –
    Take courage, man! Here – (*Giving him the golden cup.*)
    Drink, and drown thy fears in Gascon wine.

SHERASMIN (*trembling*):   An' it please your fairyship, I'm not at all thirsty; and if I were, I have no skill to drink from an empty cup. (*Aside.*) Gascon wine, indeed! A pretty Gascon tale to tell a man!

OBERON: Still faithless – still afraid! Quick – to thy mouth –

SHERASMIN: Ye – ye – yes. (*Aside.*) Heaven preserve me!'
                            (*Puts the cup to his lips.*)

OBERON: Be to thyself but true, it will not fail. (*The cup fills with wine.*) How sayst thou now?

SHERASMIN (*after a hearty draught*):   Right Gascon, by the mass! S'life! I feel quite another creature; I'm as bold as a lion! O sweet fairy!

OBERON:
    Keep thou the cup; its golden round will yield
    Pure wine, fresh springing from a thousand veins,
    If touch'd by guiltless mouth; but if base lip
    Profane its sacred brim, 'tis void, and burns
    Like molten lead the guilty wretch who grasps it.
    Now, Huon, haste where love and beauty call:
    Be bold, be constant, and be happy.

OBERON *waves his wand;* FAIRIES *appear to the symphony.*

CHORUS

FAIRIES: Honour and joy to the true and the brave,
    A friend they shall find in the elfin king;
  But, oh! to the traitor, the coward, the slave,
    For ever the fairy's curse shall cling.

SIR HUON (*to* OBERON):
  Deign, fair spirit, my steps to guide
    To the foot of the unbeliever's throne;
  There let my arm and my heart be tried,
    There be the truth of thy Huon known.

OBERON: The sun is kissing the purple tide
    That flows round my fairy bowers;
  Oft must he set in those waters wide,
    Ere mortal knight from their shore could ride
    To Bagdad's distant tow'rs.
  But, lo! I wave my lily wand,
    Once, twice, three times o'er thee,
  On the banks of the Tigris thou dost stand,
    And Bagdad is before thee.

The scene changes to the banks of the Tigris, with the city of Bagdad in the distance.

SHERASMIN: By St Denis, but he's right!

SIR HUON: Can I trust my startled sight?
  Yes, the gilded domes are there,
    In the last bright sunbeams glowing;
  And the river broad and fair
    Swiftly to the sea is flowing!
  But where, alas! is she who shed
    Love's own light upon my slumbers?
  Is that form for ever fled,
    Hush'd for aye those magic numbers?

OBERON: Grieve not, Sir Knight; but bold in glory's chase,
  Go forth; the living maid in Babylon embrace.

FAIRIES: Speed, Huon, speed; love and renown
  Soon shall thy courage and constancy crown.

         (FAIRIES *disappear*.)

OBERON *waves his wand; the bank changes to a car, drawn by swans;* OBERON *gets into it, ascends, and disappears.*

SHERASMIN (*after a pause, during which* SIR HUON *and he appear lost in wonder*): Master! are you awake, master? If your eyes be wide open, I pray you shake me, that I may open mine, too. I would fain be assured whether I be really bewitched or no.

SIR HUON: I hear the murmur of the waves; I feel the evening breeze upon my cheek. Will that foaming river, those glittering minarets, vanish in their turn?

SHERASMIN: I would wager my wits that they do, and no bad stake neither; for I know not how I shall save them otherwise, an' the fairies serve me another trick of this kidney. Now any one would swear this were a cup I hold in my hand; and I dream'd but now I drank out of it; I should like to dream that dream again – but 'tis empty; – see, see, it fills, master, it fills! (*Puts it to his mouth.*) O kind fairy! dainty Oberon! Better wine was never tasted.

BABEKAN (*without*):   Oh save me! Help! help! save me!

SIR HUON: Hark! what cry was that? Ha! look, Sherasmin!

SHERASMIN (*looking out*):   A single horseman attacked by a lion!

SIR HUON: He has fastened on the steed – it falls! – Draw, knave, and save the rider.

SHERASMIN *puts down the cup and exit with* SIR HUON. BABEKAN *enters and sinks terrified on the ground.* SHERASMIN *and* SIR HUON *re-enter, hasten to him, and raise him.*

SHERASMIN: Art hurt, man? Cheerly, cheerly! Marry, thou hadst an ugly customer to deal with there. (*Aside to* SIR HUON.) Master, this man has a most villainously looking heathen habit. If we be out of fairyland, I trow we be near Bagdad in good earnest. (*Aloud to* BABEKAN.) What! shaking still? Nay then, here's what will cure thee, (*takes up the cup*), I warrant me. Drink man, and praise the power who sent us here to save thee. (*Putting the cup to his lips.*)

BABEKAN (*screaming and dashing the cup on the ground*):   Hah! Tortures! Slave of Eblis, my lips are scorched to cinders – Curse thee, and –

SIR HUON: Hold, blasphemer! The knave meant well; – 'tis thine own guilt hath turned the wine to fire.

BABEKAN: Dog of a Frank! here come my scattered train; their scimitars shall teach thee manners.

Enter FOUR SARACENS, *armed.*

Upon them, slaves!

SARACENS *attack* SIR HUON *and* SHERASMIN.

SIR HUON: Ha! France! Ha! St Denis!

SHERASMIN: Guienne! Guienne for the noble duke!

While SIR HUON *and* SHERASMIN *defend themselves against the* SARACENS, BABEKAN *steals behind* SIR HUON *and attempts to stab him in the back,* SHERASMIN *perceives him, and strikes the weapon from his hand.* BABEKAN *and his attendants fly, pursued by* SIR HUON *and* SHERASMIN.

Scene II

The interior of NAMOUNA's *cottage.*

Enter NAMOUNA.

NAMOUNA: So, so, so, – a fine piece of news I've picked up at the palace this evening, – A pretty panic Bagdad will be in tomorrow, if the wind still blows from the same quarter, – Ul! Ul! Ul! What freaks young women take in their heads, – their heads, forsooth! young women have no heads! they think in their hearts! they are led by their hearts! and when they lose their hearts, their wits are gone into the bargain, – A plain proof – a plain proof, – Holy Prophet! talking of heads, some will be in jeopardy tomorrow, I fancy. Should the princess keep in her present mood, the caliph will make heads as cheap as turnips, before the sun goes down again.

(*A knocking without.*)

Who is there, I wonder? (*Opens the door.*)

Enter SIR HUON *and* SHERASMIN.

SHERASMIN: A word, good mother, an' it like you.

NAMOUNA: Allah guard us! What would ye, strangers?

SHERASMIN: Don't be frightened, good mother. – We are only two poor travellers, who would fain inquire where we may lodge in this strange town. We have had a long journey, – (*aside*) jump, I should say – (*aloud*) and need rest and refreshment.

NAMOUNA: 'Tis a good step to the nearest caravanserai, and I question then if you don't find it full. But, if you are not too proud, this is my humble dwelling; and if a plain, wholesome supper may content you, and clean straw till the morning, you can then look for a better lodging by daylight.

SIR HUON: Thou sayst well, dame: we will be thy guests this night.

SHERASMIN (*aside*):   A better lodging! ay, and a prettier landlady; or we're come a long way to little purpose.

NAMOUNA: Enough, Sir Stranger; I'll spread for supper directly.

(*Exit.*)

SHERASMIN: Master, I would this good dame could tell us who the craven caitiff might be, that would have murdered you out of pure gratitude for saving his worthless life from the lion, and then fled as nimbly from us, as he did from the beast before.

SIR HUON: His dress and attendants bespeak him of rank, but his deeds had shamed the poorest serf that ever tended swine.

Re-enter NAMOUNA, *with a lamp*.

NAMOUNA: Now, an' it please you, walk this way. Some milk, and a few figs, with a plate of rice, or so, is all I have to offer you; but you must make up for it at the feast tomorrow.

SIR HUON: The feast! what feast?

NAMOUNA: What feast? Why, was it not for the feast ye came to Bagdad then? The wedding feast, to be sure. Is not the caliph's daughter to be married tomorrow?

SIR HUON: The caliph's daughter! to whom, good mother, I pray you?

NAMOUNA: Why, by what road came you hither, Sir Stranger, that the tidings have not reached your ears? The whole country round rings with them.

SHERASMIN: We came by a short cut – a byroad: we travelled too fast to pick up much intelligence. On with thy tale.

NAMOUNA: Marry then, stranger, the bridegroom is Prince Babekan. He's as rich as the sea, and plays at chess better than any man in Bagdad.

SHERASMIN (*aside*): Does he? An' our knight's move do not puzzle him, say I know nothing of the game, that's all.

NAMOUNA: Ah! and a good-looking man too; in short, a prince whom all confess born for our Reiza; but, between you and I, the princess would rather marry a dragon.

SIR HUON: Ha! sayst thou?

SHERASMIN: Marry a dragon! S'death! that would be getting a check *mate*.

NAMOUNA: I say it again, sir, a dragon. Ay, ay, you may well stare; but I know what I know. There may be no feast tomorrow after all. I – I had it in confidence, and promised not to breathe a syllable; but as you are strangers, and look as if you might be trusted, I'll tell you all about it. You wonder, no doubt, how a poor old fool, like me should learn such state secrets, for the Commander of the Faithful himself knows it not as yet. One word will explain all. My granddaughter is the princess's favourite attendant.

SIR HUON: 'Tis well; but your story.

NAMOUNA: Well, well, I'm coming to it. Everybody knows that, for some time past, the caliph has been looking out for a husband for the beautiful Reiza. Offers were made in plenty, but the princess treated every suitor with the most perfect indifference. Among them came Prince Babekan, who fared no better than the rest, but the caliph, taking a great fancy to him, told the princess that, as she would not choose for herself, he must e'en choose for her, and, as she loved nobody better, she might as well marry Prince Babekan; to this, at first, she made no violent objection, but within these few hours a wonderful change has taken place, and – would you believe it! all on account of a dream.

SIR HUON AND SHERASMIN: A dream!

NAMOUNA: Ay, a dream. She fancied she was transformed to a hind, and that Prince Babekan hunted her through a forest, when suddenly a young knight, whose strange arms showed him not of eastern birth, appeared, and saved her from the darts of the huntsmen. And now, though the preparations are completed for the banquet, and the ceremony is to take place tomorrow, she has sworn never to be the bride of any one but this phantom knight; and, holy Allah! when the caliph shall hear –

SIR HUON (*with ardour*): It matters not! The lady shall keep her vow; the knight will mar the feasting else, I promise thee!

NAMOUNA: The Prophet preserve us! What do I hear? (*Viewing* SIR HUON *from head to foot.*) And what do I see! An armed knight, too! – Habit as strange as his speech! Allah il Allah! Your pardon for a moment, – I – I'll be back anon. – You'll find supper laid within. – (*Aside.*) I must to the palace as fast as my old limbs will carry me.

(*Exit hastily.*)

SHERASMIN: The old hag will raise the city on us!

SIR HUON: Fear not! She works the will of fate, and fate is friendly to us! O Sherasmin, the beautiful vision which the fairy raised was no delusion. – Such a being lives, and for me!

SHERASMIN: The caliph's daughter too! the very woman the emperor named for your bride! An' a fool might advise, Sir, I would cut the matter as short as possible. – You are commanded to kill the man who sits on the left of the caliph, and marry the princess. – Stick to the latter part of the promise, and forget the rest, master mine! Slicing off a head is but a bad preface to courtship. – Let the infidel 'scape free, and cleave to the lady. – I'll have every thing prepared for flight, and –

SIR HUON: Knave, I have pledged my knightly word to Charlemagne, and must redeem it to the letter. – Huon beyond his life, – beyond his love, – esteems his honour!

GRAND SCENA

SIR HUON: *Recitative*

Yes! even Love to Fame must yield;
   No carpet Knight am I:
My home it is the battle field –
   My song the battle cry!

Air

O 'tis a glorious sight to see
The charge of the Christian chivalry,
When thundering over the ground they go,
Their lances levell'd in long, long row!

One shock, and those lances are shiver'd all,
   But they shiver not in vain –
They have raised for the foe a rampart wall
   With the bodies of the slain!

On they spur over dying and dead –
Swords are flashing round ev'ry head –
They are raised again, but they glitter no more,
Ev'ry blade is dimm'd with gore!
The fight is done! – The field is won! –
Their trumpets startle the sinking sun!
As the night winds whirl the red leaves afar,
They have scatter'd the might of the Moslemah!
Mourn ye maidens of Palestine,
Your lovers lie stark in the cold moonshine
The eyes ye kiss'd ere ye bade them go,
Are food for the kite, and hooded crow!
Joy to the high-born dame of France!

Conquest waits on her warrior's lance!
Joy to the girls of fair Guienne!
Their lovers are hast'ning home again!
Hark! they come! the brave ones see,
Who have humbled the pride of Paynimrie,

    Twine the wreath, the feast prepare,
    Fill to the brim the goblet fair;
    Strike the harp; – and loud and high,
    Swell the song of Victory!

(*Exeunt.*)

Scene III

Vestibule in the haram, looking on the Tigris, which is seen by moonlight through a balustrade in the background.

Enter REIZA, *followed by* FATIMA.

REIZA: Name not the prince, dear Fatima. I hate, I loathe him! Wed *him*! I would wed a serpent sooner! Since the wretch hath harbour'd in this court, I scarcely recognize my father, – O Fatima! what a hapless lot is ours, – shut up in this splendid prison, no liberty but that of thought, which cannot be debarred us, but which only serves to aggravate the sense of our misfortune. – The slaves, the toys, of a sex that despises us, – Our very lives dependent upon the caprice of a tyrant! Surely, surely, in those western climes, to which the sun hastens every evening, as though he loved to look on them, woman's fate must be a fairer one! Ah! do not, I beseech thee, friend, strive to crush the solitary hope, which saves me from madness! Trust to my heart's fond bodings. – The knight of my dream, – my destined lord – is near me, and will break this dreadful bondage.

FATIMA: How can the daughter of the mighty Haroun suffer an idle vision to get the better of her judgement? Let my mistress listen to the words of her slave.

REIZA: Fatima, dear Fatima! – How often must I pray thee not to address me in the language of servitude. Thou art my companion, my friend! The slavish phrases of our eastern tongue were from childhood unpleasing to me, and now, methinks, they sound more vilely than ever. – The elected of my heart is a Frank – a Christian. – The same power which raised his form to my sight hath also whispered truths in mine ear, which I fear to repeat even to thee, my Fatima! And canst thou speak of such a vision, as of an ordinary dream? No, no; be sure it is the work of fate. The hour draws nigh! The chains already sound! – But think not I will wear them. If this heart be indeed deceived, I have yet a hope in store, which cannot fail. – Yes, Fatima! (*In a low but determined tone, and half drawing her dagger.*) Love or death shall free me!

FATIMA: Merciful Allah! sheathe that dreadful weapon! (*Knocking without.*) Hark! hark, lady! someone knocks at the little door that opens on the private passage, but I dare not leave you in this desperate mood.

REIZA: Fear nothing, girl! The time hath not yet arrived, – I will act
firmly, but not rashly. (*Knocking again.*) They are impatient, – away,
and see who knocks. (*Exit* FATIMA.) No, no; – my hope of happiness
is yet too strong for me, to rush undriven, on so stern an alternative!

FINALE

Recitative

REIZA: Haste, gallant knight! Oh, haste and save
      Thy Reiza from the yawning grave!
      For round this hand the worm shall twine,
      Ere linked in other grasp than thine!

Air

      Yes, – my lord! – my joy! – my blessing!
        Reiza lives for thee alone!
      On this heart his signet pressing,
        Love hath claimed it for thine own!
      Yes, its core thine image beareth,
        There it must for ever burn,
      Like the spot the tulip weareth
        Deep within its dewy urn!*

Re-enter FATIMA, *hastily*.

Recitative

FATIMA: Joy! – we are rescued in the hour of need!
      Joy! he is found! – the knight is ours indeed!

REIZA: Found! where? Sweet Fatima, ah, quickly tell!

FATIMA: To old Namouna's cot, as evening fell,
      He came, by fate directed: there he heard
      Thy dream, as I had told her, – word for word, –
      And vowed, with glowing cheek and flashing eye,
      To rescue thee or die.

REIZA (*exultingly*):
      Said I not?

FATIMA: Ah! happy maid!

Duo – REIZA *and* FATIMA.

REIZA: Near $\left\{ \begin{array}{l} \text{me} \\ \text{thee} \end{array} \right\}$ is $\left\{ \begin{array}{l} \text{my} \\ \text{thy} \end{array} \right\}$ own true knight!

      Hope hath not $\left\{ \begin{array}{l} \text{my} \\ \text{thy} \end{array} \right\}$ heart betray'd!

      Love hath read the dream aright!

---

  * 'La tulippe est chez eux (les Persans et les Turcs) le symbole d'un amant passionné,
a cause que cette fleur a ordinairement ses feuilles rouges, et qu'elle est marquée au fond
d'une noirceur qui a quelque resemblance à la marque que laisse l'application ou l'impres-
sion d'un baton de feu. Ainsi, disent ils, l'amant a le feu sur le visage, et la blessure
dans le cœur'. (D'Herbelot, *Bib. Orient. Art. Laleh.*)

FATIMA: Hark, lady, hark! On the terrace near,
                 The tread of the haram guard I hear –
                 And lo! thy slaves that hither hie,
                 Show that the hour of rest is nigh.

REIZA *and* FATIMA *interchange signs of secrecy. A band of black and white*
slaves enter from the gardens, headed by MESROUR *and female slaves of the*
princess.

REIZA: Oh, my wild, exulting soul!
                 How shall I thy joy control?
                 My kindling eye, my burning cheek,
                 Far, oh! far too plainly speak.
                 Ere thy tumult they betray,
                 Let me hence! – Away! Away!
                              Chorus
                 Now the evening watch is set,
                 And from ev'ry minaret
                 Soon the Muezzin's call to prayer
                 Will sweetly float on the quiet air.

                 Here no later must $\left\{\begin{matrix} ye \\ we \end{matrix}\right\}$ stray,

                 Hence, to rest – Away! Away!

ACT II

Scene I

A magnificent banqueting hall in the palace of HAROUN. *On a divan at the back of the scene, the* CALIPH *is discovered seated. On his left hand is* PRINCE BABEKAN. *On each side of the divan hangs a rich veil, behind which are supposed to be the apartments of the females. Embroidered carpets are spread before the* CALIPH *and the* PRINCE, *and on them gilt trays are seen, filled with fruit, coffee, sherbets, &c. The great officers of the* CALIPH's *court, black and white eunuchs, &c. form a line on each side of the stage.*

CHORUS

> Glory to the caliph! to Haroun the Just!
> Bow, ye true believers, before him to the dust.
> Woe betide the infidel who dares the caliph's might,
> When on the breeze he floating sees
> 'The shadow and the night!'★

CALIPH (*to attendants*):   Peace. Prince (*to* BABEKAN), the hour is arrived, which, my astrologers have assured me, is marked upon the table of light as the one destined by Allah for the marriage of our daughter Reiza.

PRINCE: Commander of the Faithful! The impatience of Babekan is at its height. May it please you to give order for the instant solemnization of our nuptials?

CALIPH: Bring forth the bride –

Music. The veil on the right of the CALIPH *is withdrawn, and a train of dancing girls enter, preceding the* PRINCESS, *who, veiled and richly attired for the ceremony, advances, supported by* FATIMA *and followed by the female slaves of the haram.*

REIZA (*aside to* FATIMA):   He is not here! Should he desert me now –
(*Gazes round her in great agitation, and grasps the hilt of her dagger.*)

FATIMA (*alarmed*): Lady, he will not. Be of good cheer, sweet mistress –

CALIPH: Daughter, approach! (*Clashing of swords without.*)
> Hah! the clash of swords! Head of my father!
> What desperate slaves are these?

★ Two black banners, so called, of the Caliphs of the House of Abbas.

Enter SIR HUON *and* SHERASMIN, *swords in hand.*

SIR HUON: Where is my love? my bride,

REIZA: Ah! 'tis he! save me! save me!

> (*Rushes into* SIR HUON'*s arms.*)

SIR HUON (*kissing her*):   Thus, thus thy Huon claims thee for his own!

CALIPH: Am I awake? Slaves! Dogs! Hew him in pieces!

BABEKAN (*to the guards*):   Hold! mighty caliph! be mine that task.
(*Drawing his scimitar, and rushing on* SIR HUON.)

SIR HUON (*disengaging himself from* REIZA):   Ha! Is it thou that sittest
upon the caliph's left? Fortune, I thank thee! Die, unbelieving
traitor! (*Cuts him down.*)

CALIPH (*stamping with fury*):   Allah il Allah! Tear out his heart!

The slaves, who have stood as if thunderstruck by the temerity of SIR HUON,
at this command rush towards him.

SHERASMIN (*to* SIR HUON, *quickly*):   Master! the horn! the horn!

SIR HUON *winds the horn: all except himself and* SHERASMIN *stand motionless
in their various attitudes.*

SIR HUON: Thanks, Oberon! Cæsar, I have fulfilled my promise! –
Haste, Sherasmin, – the power of the spell extends throughout the
palace! While it lasts, let us secure the princess.

> (*Exit, bearing out* REIZA.)

SHERASMIN: And the waiting maid into the bargain. – Up and away,
my pretty pagan! Like master, like man, say I – and a nicer little
armful never fell to the lot of a Frank. – Don't stir, my good friends,
I entreat – I couldn't think of troubling you.

> (*Exit, bearing out* FATIMA.)

Scene II

The palace gardens.

Enter FOUR SARACENS (*the same as in Act I.*)

FIRST SARACEN: Prithee, no more of thy foolery, Amrou; the blows
thou didst take from those Christian dogs last night have left such
a singing in thine ears that thou art incapable of understanding a
plain tale and dost confound accounts most vilely. – What possible
relation can exist between those miserable infidels and the daughter
of the Commander of the Faithful?

SECOND SARACEN: That I know not. All I say is, that there is a rumour
throughout the city of a Frankish enchanter who has cast a spell
upon the princess and has vowed to carry her off on a fiery dragon,
and –

FIRST SARACEN: Peace – look yonder – what be they, hurrying hither-
ward, with each a woman in his arms?

SECOND SARACEN: The two infidels, by the beard of the Prophet!

FIRST SARACEN: Amrou! Ali! let us behind these bushes. Be he Eblis himself, I'll be revenged on that foremost dog for the panic he put me in yesterday –

SECOND SARACEN: Quick! Quick! We are four to two, and the guard within call. They cannot escape – unless they be devils indeed.

(*They retire.*)

Enter SIR HUON *and* SHERASMIN *hastily – bearing* REIZA *and* FATIMA.

SIR HUON (*stopping*):   We have taken the wrong path. This leads us back to the palace.

SHERASMIN: No, no, Sir. We are right enough – forward! forward!

The SARACENS *rush from their hiding place and seize* SIR HUON *and* SHERASMIN.

FIRST SARACEN: We have the slaves! What ho! there – a guard! a guard!

SECOND SARACEN: Hold him fast – (*Snatching the magic horn.*) Here's that shall bring assistance. (*Blows a furious blast.*)

Violent thunder and lightning – the SARACENS *fly in terror – the stages fills with clouds, which open in the centre, and* OBERON *appears –* REIZA *and* FATIMA *start from their trance.*

OBERON (*to* SIR HUON):

   Huon, thou hast redeem'd thy knightly pledge,
   And I am well content. The maid is thine!
   Yet ere thou waft her from her native shore, –
   Speak, Reiza! Dost thou willingly forego
   Pomp, riches, pow'r, thy native court and throne,
   To be the bride of a young wand'ring knight,
   To love but him alone, and with him share
   Each stern vicissitude his fate may know?
   Reflect, ere yet too late. If this alarm thee,
   Bid love's delusive visions melt away,
   And at my word, the past no longer known,
   The caliph shall again his child embrace,
   And Reiza, great and glorious as before,
   Shall reign the queen of Fars and Araby.

REIZA: King of the Genii! for sure thou art no less! thy piercing eye can read my heart, and witness to the truth of my tongue. Come weal, come woe, Reiza will love and follow this valiant knight throughout the world, so he will prove as true!

SIR HUON: Else may all good desert me.

OBERON: Enough!

Waves his wand. The clouds disperse and discover the seashore, with the port of Ascalon: a vessel lying at anchor.

   Behold the port of Ascalon!
   Yon bark is bound for Greece. Hie thee on board.
   Whate'er may hap, remember Oberon
   Befriends ye, whilst his friendship you deserve.
   Farewell! Be true, and triumph! (OBERON *vanishes.*)

(*Exeunt* SIR HUON *and* REIZA.)

SHERASMIN (*to* FATIMA): Don't be frighten'd, my little unbeliever. He's an old friend, bless you. He didn't ask you if you'll love me; but there's little doubt of that when we come to be better acquainted. I'll make thee a marvellous fond husband, I warrant theé.

FATIMA: I must needs trust thee, for I have no other hope to follow my lady, and I would rather thou shouldst prove a bad one than part me from her.

SHERASMIN: Why then, most faithful of infidels! thou Christian-hearted little Mohammedan! thou shalt have me by this light, for thou deserv'st me; and I am not for every woman's market, I promise thee.

FATIMA: But canst thou love one of another faith?

SHERASMIN: 'Faith can I, if she can love me; love is of all faiths.

FATIMA: And sometimes of none, in Araby. I know not if the men be truer in Frangistan –

SHERASMIN: Frangi – O – ah – I know – you mean my country. Why, my dear, for the matter of that, a – a man's a man, you know, all the world over, except when he betrays an affectionate woman; and then, curse him, he's no man.

FATIMA: Ay, that's the way you all talk at the beginning. None of you ever dream of betraying an affectionate woman, till you find the woman *is* affectionate, and then an excuse is easily found for the action. But what will your other wives say when you bring a stranger amongst them?

SHERASMIN: My other wives! O, never trouble your head about that, my love. We Franks find one wife at a time enough in all conscience.

FATIMA: One wife! how odd!

SHERASMIN: Odd! Ay, according to *your* matrimonial arithmetic, perhaps; but in my country we should call two wives the odd number; besides, we couldn't so easily get rid of a refractory spouse as your eastern husbands.

FATIMA: Do you Franks then never tie your wives up in sacks and fling them into the river?

SHERASMIN: No; nor send them bowstrings with their husband's compliments, and beg they'll be strangled immediately. But many in my country would be happy, I dare say, if you could introduce either of the customs.

FATIMA: Not I, for the world: I shall be too glad to live in a country where I need not be every moment putting my hand to my head, to feel if it be still on my shoulders.

SHERASMIN: Well, well, my little Pagan, you have nothing to fear on that score; I have lived a stout bachelor these five and thirty years in despite of all the simpers and ogles of all the girls in Gascony. But there's something in those little heathen twinklers of thine which makes me fancy I shall love thee most furiously.

FATIMA: And shall I pay visits, and make feasts, as the married women do in Bagdad?

SHERASMIN: You shall walk till you're tired, and eat as long as you're able; you shall go to court, and see the emperor; you shall go to Rome, and see the pope; bid adieu to locks, bolts and bars, palaces that are prisons, and husbands that are gaolers. We'll be contracted here by a cadi, and married at home by a monk. In less than a year you'll drink wine, and abjure the Koran; and then you and your first boy may be christened together. What sayest thou, my girl; dost think thou canst love me? Wilt thou follow me? And wilt thou follow nobody else afterwards? For such things do happen in France, once in a century or so.

FATIMA: Bless me, what a many questions you ask at a time; I hardly know how to answer you. But, I think I may promise.

SONG

FATIMA: A lonely Arab maid,
                  The desert's simple child,
            Unskilled in arts, by which, 'tis said,
                  Man's love may be beguil'd,
            Like some uprooted flow'r am I,
                  Upon a river flung,
            To float a little hour, then die,
                  Unheeded as I sprung.

            But if thy friendly hand
                  Should lift me from the tide
            And bear me to some distant land,
                  To bloom, thy bosom's pride;
            O, sooner from his darling rose
                  The nightingale shall roam,
            Than I disturb that heart's repose,
                  Which love hath made my home.

SHERASMIN: Enough, my little warbler, thou art mine. This kiss to seal the bargain. By my faith, thou art the rose and the nightingale blended that thou sing'st of. An' my master be as well pleased as I am, there are not two happier fellows in Christendom.

Re-enter SIR HUON *and* REIZA, *with the captain of the vessel.*

SIR HUON: Now, Sherasmin, to the port. The wind is fair for Greece. The captain here stays for us. Dear Reiza, I burn to kneel with thee before the throne of Charlemagne! That sweet revenge is all I ask of heaven!

QUARTETTO (SIR HUON, CAPTAIN, REIZA *and* FATIMA)

SIR HUON AND CAPTAIN:
                  Over the dark blue waters,
                        Over the wide, wide sea,
                  Fairest of Araby's daughters,
                        Say, wilt thou sail with me?

REIZA AND FATIMA:
>Were there no bounds to the water,
>>No shore to the wide, wide sea,
>Still fearless would Araby's daughter
>>Sail on through life with thee.

ALL:
>On board then, on board, while the skies are light,
>>And friendly blows the gale;
>Our hearts are as true as our bark, and bright
>>Our hopes as its sunlit sail!

(*Exeunt.*)

Scene IV* Rocks

Enter PUCK.

PUCK:
>Here, by Oberon's command,
>Have I flown from fairy land,
>Ere to earth a dewy gem
>Could drop from a rose's diadem;
>Gifted with his power to call
>Those whose art may raise a squall,
>Which shall make old ocean roll,
>Foaming in his rocky bowl,
>Till in wrath he piecemeal tear
>The bark which beareth yonder pair,
>And fling them on the island nigh;
>First trial of their constancy.

Sings

>Spirits of air, and earth, and sea,
>Spirits of fire, which holy be,
>All that have power o'er wind and wave,
>Come hither, come hither, my spirits so brave.
>Whether ye be in the cavern dark,
>Lighted alone by the diamond spark,
>Or beneath the waters deep,
>Where the prisoned pearl doth sleep,
>Or in skies beyond the one
>Mortal eyes do look upon,
>Or in the womb of some groaning hill,
>Where the lava stream is boiling still, –
>Spirits, wherever ye chance to be,
>Come hither, come hither, come hither to me;
>I charge ye by the magic ring
>Of your faithful friend, the fairy king.

SPIRITS *appear in various parts of the stage.*

Chorus of SPIRITS

>We are here! we are here!
>>Say, what must be done?
>Must we cleave the moon's sphere?
>>Must we darken the sun?

---

* In the 1826 edition of Planché's *Oberon* scene IV followed scene II. We have left this unchanged.

Must we empty the ocean upon its own shore?
Speak! speak! we have pow'r to do this and more!

Recitative

PUCK: Nay, nay, your task will be, at most,
          To wreck a bark upon this coast,
          Which simple fairy may not do,
          And therefore have I summon'd you!

Chorus of SPIRITS

Naught but that? Ho, ho, ho, ho!
Lighter labour none we know.
Winds and waves obey the spell:
Hark! 'tis done! Farewell! farewell!

Thunder and lightning. PUCK *and* SPIRITS *vanish.*

Scene V

Cavern on the sea beach. The ocean seen through the mouth of it. Other perforations lead through the rock to the interior of the island. Storm continued. Stage very dark: fragments of wreck are thrown upon the stage.

Enter SIR HUON, *supporting* REIZA, *who is nearly exhausted.*

SIR HUON: Look up, my love! my wife! O heaven, she dies! My Reiza
            dies! And I – I am her murderer! – 'Twas for my sake she gave up
            every thing – a throne! – a father! – O spare her, gracious heaven!

AIR

SIR HUON: Ruler of this awful hour,
            Spare! oh, spare yon tender flow'r!
            If thou must strike, oh, let thy thunder fall
            On me! on me! the wretched cause of all!

REIZA (*recovering*):   Huon!

SIR HUON: Ah! she speaks! she speaks! But wretch that I am! Where
            shall I find food and shelter for her on this frightful shore? O my
            sweet bride! To see thee thus forlorn and desolate, and know myself
            the cause, drives me to madness!

REIZA: Dearest Huon, do not speak thus. If I must die, it is enough
         that I breathe my last upon thy bosom.

SIR HUON: My fond, true girl! – this kindness but augments my agony!
            That such should be the fate of love like thine! O Oberon! is this
            thy friendship? Cruel spirit! no help! no – (*The waves cast the magic
            cup on shore.*) Hah! can it be? (*Snatching it up, and putting it to his lips*).
            It is! It is the magic cup! Forgive me, fairy! Drink, drink, sweet
            Reiza; for thee its richest stream will surely flow?

REIZA (*after having drank*):   O cheering draught! thy power is great
         indeed; I feel new strength; new hope thrill through my veins. Dear
         Huon, a wonder chained our hearts together, and wonders still
         surround us. Yes, these are but trials surely, and though severe they
         be, will end in happiness.

SIR HUON: I must needs think so, but alas! this cup! where is its faithful bearer? My poor varlet! my trusty Sherasmin! drowned! drowned!

REIZA: And Fatima, the kind, devoted Fatima, she, too I fear, hath perished. Thou and I alone have 'scaped the general wreck!

SIR HUON: Not so. The heartless captain and his crew took to the boats. Despairing then, I plunged with thee into the waves, followed by Sherasmin with Fatima; and from that moment I saw them no more.

REIZA: Unfortunates!

SIR HUON: But what must now be done? The storm is abating, as if satisfied with the destruction it hath made: this cavern is dry and overgrown with moss. What if thou shouldst rest thee here while I ascend the cliffs, and look around to see if aught like human aid be near us?

REIZA: Be it so. But stay not long from me.

SIR HUON: I will not, sweetest. Ah! where is now the ivory horn that would have brought us succour instantly?

(*Exit* SIR HUON.)

GRAND SCENA

Recitative

REIZA: Ocean! Thou mighty monster that liest curled,
Like a green serpent, round about the world!
To musing eye thou art an awful sight,
When calmly sleeping in the morning light;
But when thou risest in thy wrath, as now,
And fling'st thy folds around some fated prow,
Crushing the strong-ribbed bark as 'twere a reed,
Then, Ocean, art thou terrible indeed!

Air

Still I see thy billows flashing,
Through the gloom their white foam flinging,
And the breaker's sullen dashing
In mine ear hope's knell is ringing!
But lo! methinks a light is breaking
Slowly o'er the distant deep,
Like a second morn awaking,
Pale and feeble from its sleep!
Brighter now, behold, 'tis beaming
On the storm whose misty train
Like some shatter'd flag is streaming,
Or a wild steed's flying mane!

Recitative

And now the sun bursts forth! the wind is lulling fast,
And the broad wave but pants from fury past!

Air

Cloudless o'er the blushing water,
Now the setting sun is burning!
Like a victor red with slaughter,
To his tent in triumph turning!
Ah! perchance these eyes may never
Look upon his light again!
Fare thee well, bright orb, for ever!
Thou for me wilt rise in vain!
But what gleams so white and fair,
Heaving with the heaving billow?
'Tis a seabird wheeling there
O'er some wretch's wat'ry pillow!
No! it is no bird I mark.
Joy! it is a boat! a sail!
And yonder rides a gallant bark
Uninjured by the gale!
O transport! my Huon! haste down to the shore!
Quick, quick, for a signal this scarf shall be waved!
They see me! they answer! they ply the strong oar!
My husband! my love! we are saved! we are saved!

During this Scena the storm clears off as described; the setting sun breaks forth in full splendour; a small boat is seen, and immediately afterwards a large vessel. Towards the conclusion of the Scena, the boat disappears as making in for the shore.

REIZA: Huon! Huon! why tarriest thou? See, they near the beach! they leap into the surf – they come!

Enter ABDALLAH *and Pirates.*

ABDALLAH: Hah! A fair prize, by Mahomet! Seize her, my lads, and away to sea again: she's worth a fortune to us!

(*They seize her.*)

REIZA: What mean ye, strangers? I cannot go alone! One dear to me as life is ranging o'er the cliffs; but he will return speedily. Huon – Huon!

ABDALLAH: *He* will return! It's a man then. No, no, my Peri! we have neither time to wait his return, nor wish for his company. The market's overstocked with male rubbish. Thou art just the bale of goods we were looking for. To the boat with her!

REIZA: Ah! Huon! Huon! save me! help! help!

SIR HUON *rushes in.*

HUON: Madness and misery! villains, release her!

ABDALLAH: Down with the dog!

SIR HUON *is struck to the ground senseless.*

ABDALLAH (*raising his sword to plunge into his bosom*):   Die!

REIZA (*breaking from the grasp of the Pirates, and flinging herself before* SIR HUON):   Mercy! Mercy!

ABDALLAH: Dost thou plead for him? Well, 'twere almost a pity to stain a good Damascus blade with the blood of so sorry a slave as this. So I'll be merciful for once. Bind him and leave him to his fate. He'll starve and rot; and there's an ablution saved. Away with her to the boat.

REIZA: O horrible! Leave him not to perish here alone! If ye be men, have pity on us both: sell us for slaves, but do not separate us!

ABDALLAH: To the boat I say!

They drag off REIZA, *while another party bind the arms of* SIR HUON, *who remains insensible.*

As soon as they have quitted the stage, a symphony is heard. OBERON *descends in a car drawn by swans.*

OBERON (*descending from the car*):
   Alas! poor mortal! Oberon deplores
   The cruel fate which bids him to the quick
   Probe the hurt spirit of a child of clay,
   So free from all the leaven of his race!
   But keep thou true; and once thy trials o'er,
   Thy fairy friend, released from his rash vow,
   Shall pay thee, for each moment past of pain,
   Years of high honour and unfading love!
   (*Stamping*) Puck! my brave spirit!

PUCK (*appearing*):
   Here, great Oberon!

OBERON:
   Servant, here is more to do;
   Thou must guard this child of clay
   From the night's unwholesome dew,
   From the scorching beams of day,
   'Till yon sun, about to set,
   Hath seven times the waters met;
   For when seven days have past,
   The Pirate shall his anchor cast
   In Tunis' bay. Then through the air,
   As quick as light this mortal bear,
   And lay him gently down before
   Old Ibrahim the gard'ner's door.
   Lo! upon his lids I shed
   Sleep like that which binds the dead.
   Sound nor shock the spell shall break,
   'Till thou in Tunis bid him wake.

PUCK:
   Mighty king of fairy land,
   Be it as thou dost command,
   Him to shield from sun and shower,
   Puck will build a fairy bow'r
   Here upon this desert shore,
   Where never flow'ret bloomed before.

Waves his wand. A pavilion of flowers rises and encloses SIR HUON. *The sun sets, and the stars appear.*

>See – 'tis done: nor noxious dew
>Nor scorching ray shall pierce it through,
>Though ev'ry gentle beam and air
>May freely find an entrance there.
>But master! mark where in the sky
>The night star opes its silver eye,
>The herald of the lady moon,
>Whose light will gladden the waters soon!
>And hark! – The mermaids 'witching strain
>Steals o'er the lull'd and list'ning main!

FINALE

FIRST MERMAID *sings* (*within*)

>O 'tis pleasant to float on the sea,
>When the wearied waves in a deep sleep be,
>And the last faint light of the sun hath fled,
>And the stars are mustering over head,
>And the night breeze comes with its breath so bland,
>Laden with sweets from the distant land!
>O! 'tis pleasant to float and sing,
>While ever our dripping locks we wring!

SECOND MERMAID *sings*

>O! 'tis pleasant to float on the sea,
>When nothing stirs on its breast but we!
>The warder leans at the twilight hour
>Over the wall of his time-worn tow'r,
>And signs himself, and mutters a pray'r,
>Then listens again to the 'witching air!
>O! 'tis pleasant to float and sing,
>While ever our dripping locks we wring!

Recitative

PUCK: Master! say – our toil is o'er,
>May we dance upon this shore?
>And a merry burden bear
>To the mermaids' ditty rare?

OBERON: Better boon thy zeal hath won;
>I will stay and see it done.

Duetto

OBERON AND PUCK:
>Hither! hither! ye elfin throng,
>Come dance on the sands to the mermaids' song;
>Hasten and prove to the nymphs of the sea,
>That the spirits of earth can as jocund be,
>Come as lightly, and look as fair,
>As blossoms that sail on the summer air.

Hither! hither! ye elfin throng,
Come dance on the sands to the mermaids' song.

During the duet the stage becomes illuminated by the light of the moon.
MERMAIDS *and* WATER NYMPHS *appear on the sea, and* FAIRIES *enter and sing the following.*

CHORUS

Who would stay in her coral cave,
When the moon shines over the quiet wave,
And the stars are studding the dark blue arch,
Through which she speeds on her nightly march.
Merrily, merrily, let us sail
Over the sea by her light so pale!

OBERON, PUCK *and* FAIRIES:

Who would sleep in the lily's bell,
When the moon shines over each wood and dell,
And the stars are studding the dark blue arch,
Through which she speeds on her nightly march.
Merrily, merrily, dance we here
Over the sands by her light so clear.

ACT III

Scene I

Exterior of IBRAHIM *the gardener's house. – Sunrise.*

Enter FATIMA, *in a slave's dress, from the house.*

FATIMA: Alas! poor Fatima, how changed is thy lot! The sun, which so lately beheld thee the favourite attendant of a mighty princess, now rises upon the lowly slave of Ibrahim, the gardener of the emir of Tunis. And that beloved mistress, where now is she? – the beautiful, the powerful, the worshipped Reiza? sunk in the merciless ocean, or perishing upon some barren rock, with the chosen of her heart, her gallant but ill-fated Huon! Yet surely that powerful spirit who professed himself so strongly their protector, cannot thus barbarously have deserted them. No, – I will cherish the hope, that we shall shortly meet again. My own unlooked for preservation may well encourage the idea. Besides, I had a dream last night, which should prognosticate good fortune.

<u>SONG</u>

FATIMA:
      O Araby! dear Araby!
        My own, my native land!
      Methought I cross'd the dark blue sea,
        And trod again thy strand.
      And there I saw my father's tent
        Beneath the tall date trees,
      And the sound of music and merriment
        Came sweetly on the breeze.
      And thus to the lightly touch'd guitar
        I heard a maiden tell
      Of one who fled from a proud Serdar,
        With the youth she loved so well.

      Al, al, al, al! though the night-star be high,
      'Tis the morning of joy for my Yusuf and I;
      Though the flow'rs of the garden have closed ev'ry one,
      The rose of the heart blooms in love's rising sun.
      Al, al, al, al! soon will Zeenab be far

From the drear Anderûn* of the cruel Serdar.
Al, al, al, al! 'tis the neigh of his steed!
O, prove, my good barb, thou art worthy thy breed!
Now o'er the salt desert we fly like the wind;
And our fears fade as fast as the turrets behind.
Al, al, al, al! we the frontier have won,
And may laugh at the lord of the drear Anderûn.

Enter SHERASMIN, *in a gardener's dress, with a spade in one hand and a basket of flowers in the other.*

SHERASMIN: Ah! Fatima, art there, my girl? Here am I, in the garb of my new occupation, you see, which I have taken to as kindly as possible, considering circumstances. Hast seen our master this morning?

FATIMA: No, but he is up, and gone into the city on some business.

SHERASMIN: He's a kind-hearted old soul, Fatima. I marked his eye twinkle when he heard the captain of the vessel, who picked us up, say, how narrowly we escaped being food for fish; and I shall never forget the tone in which he said, 'Poor devils! the waves didn't separate you, and shall I be more cruel than they? – No, there's your price, captain; and now get you two along together; work hard, feed well, and be merry!'

FATIMA: Ay, Sherasmin, it was kind indeed of him not to part us. Our lot would have been truly miserable, if destitute of that last consolation, the opportunity of deploring it together. Heaven grant that our poor lord and lady were –

SHERASMIN: Ah! that's a bad business, indeed, Fatima; but not so bad, I hope, as it seems. I cannot suppress the strong conviction, that they are safe. The magic horn, I fear, was left in the haram gardens at Bagdad, and the fairy cup is full of salt water. – But, though the gifts be lost, the giver is as powerful as ever. – So kiss thy fond husband, my girl, and a fig for misfortune. Let's make up our minds to be happy – there's a good deal in that, I can tell you – Gad, what merry days I have seen in my time, and I hope to see some more yet, Fatima.

DUET (SHERASMIN *and* FATIMA)

SHERASMIN: On the banks of sweet Garonne,
I was born one fine spring morning.
Soon as I could run alone,
Kicks, and cuffs, and tumbles scorning,
Shirking labour, loving fun,
Swigging wine, and hating water,
Fighting ev'ry neighbour's son,
And kissing ev'ry neighbour's daughter,
O how fast the days have flown
On the banks of sweet Garonne?

* The harem, or women's apartment.

FATIMA: On the waves of Bund-emir
                   First I saw the day-beam quiver;
               There I wander'd, year by year,
                   On the banks of that fair river;
               Roaming with my roaming race,
                   Wheresoe'er the date tree lured them;
               Or a greener resting place
                   Pasture for their flocks ensured them.
               Never knew I grief or fear
               On the banks of Bund-emir!

SHERASMIN: Times have alter'd, mistress mine!

FATIMA: Fled is fortune's summer weather.
    We are slaves –

SHERASMIN: Yet why repine
                   While, my dear, we're slaves together!
               Let's be merry as we're true,
                   Love our song, and Joy the chorus,
               Dig and delve, and bill and coo,
                   As Eve and Adam did before us.

BOTH: Let's be merry, & c.

(*Exeunt* FATIMA *and* SHERASMIN.)

PUCK *descends with* SIR HUON.

PUCK: Seven times hath blush'd the morn,
               Since thy love was from thee torn;
               Seven times the sun hath set,
               Since thine eyes his light hath met.
               Now in port the bark doth ride,
               Which contains thy captive bride.
               Wake! a faithful friend is nigh!
               Back to fairy land I fly!

PUCK *disappears.* SIR HUON *shows signs of returning animation.*

Re-enter SHERASMIN.

SHERASMIN: So, that's all right. – Now for – (*seeing* SIR HUON) Hollo!
    What have we here? – Eh! – No – Yes! – is it possible? my master!
    my dear master! I shall go mad with joy. (*Helping him to rise.*) Sir,
    sir! speak to me – don't you know me? It's Sherasmin, your faithful
    Sherasmin.

SIR HUON (*gazing about him wildly*):   Sherasmin! where am I? How
    came I here? What new miracle is this? Is it a dream, or did I dream
    till now?

SHERASMIN: By St Denis, master, I am as much puzzled as yourself;
    but this I know, that you are here in Tunis, before the door of old
    Ibrahim, the emir's gardener, who bought both Fatima and I in the
    slavemarket two days ago.

SIR HUON: Fatima here too!

SHERASMIN: Yes, Sir, we were picked up at sea by a corsair of Tunis, just as we were at the last gasp. But where's my lady, sir? Safe and sound, I hope, if not with you.

SIR HUON: O Sherasmin! how you rend open my wound again! Twelve hours have scarcely passed, since a band of pirates tore her from the rude rock on which the waves had cast us, and these weaponless arms, which could no longer defend her. Whither they have borne her, heaven only knows.

SHERASMIN: Twelve hours ago! – Why, master, the desert shore on which our vessel struck is full four days' sail from Tunis with the fairest wind, and –

SIR HUON: Well! it may be so – I was felled to the earth by the ruffian crew, and how long I lay senseless, I know as little as the means by which I was wafted to this spot. But doubtless Oberon hath stood my friend – and from that thought I gather new hope and courage to struggle with my fate!

SHERASMIN: I said it! I said but now to Fatima, we shall all meet again, and be merry! See, Sir, here she comes. Lord, lord, how glad she will be to see you!

Re-enter FATIMA, *hastily.*

FATIMA: Oh Sherasmin! such news! such news! (*Seeing* SIR HUON.) Ah! mercy on me! what do I see?

SHERASMIN: See! Why, you see my noble master alive and well, Fatima! – Praised by the kind fairy! I knew it. I felt it all along. I couldn't be melancholy, though I tried, and now I somehow, – I can't help crying for the life and soul of me: this turning gardener has made my head like an old watering pot.

FATIMA: And came my noble lord with my lady?

SIR HUON: Your lady! Alas! Fatima, I know not where or in whose power she pines!

FATIMA: Wonder on wonder then! – For 'twas of her I came to tell. – My lady lives – my lady is in Tunis!

SIR HUON *and* SHERASMIN: Here! in Tunis!

FATIMA: At the palace.

SIR HUON: Hast seen her, Fatima? Speak! speak, for heaven's sake!

FATIMA: No, my dear lord, I have not seen her; but this morning a bark put into Tunis, and the rumour runs that within this hour the captain has presented to the emir a most beautiful female, found on a desert island. Alamanzor was enchanted at the first glance, dismissed the captain with a magnificent present, and has lodged her in a pavilion in the haram gardens, which till now, belonged to his wife Roshana. The crew of the vessel have blazoned her beauty through the city; and from their description I have no doubt of its being the princess.

SIR HUON: 'Tis she! – my conscious heart assures me 'tis my Reiza! Your counsel, my kind friends: what's to be done?

SHERASMIN: Mortal force will avail us nothing, and we have no magic

horn to aid us as at Bagdad. – Our first care must be to establish
you, unsuspected, in this neighbourhood. Oh! we'll patch up a story
never fear – I will pray Ibrahim to take you also into his service,
and if I succeed you must e'en be content to dig beside your poor
Sherasmin, till time and fate shall favour our enterprise. Come in,
sir; – the old man is from home at present – and ere he return, we
must manage to equip you in a less suspicious habit than that. But
stay – yonder comes a Greek – a fellow servant of ours, who is as
anxious to get out of the clutches of the infidels as we are. The varlet
has all the cunning of his country – I'll just let him into as much of
your situation as 'tis fit he should know, and he'll help me to patch
up a story, I warrant you!

Enter ARCON.

SHERASMIN *takes him aside, and during the commencement of the Trio converses
with him in dumb show.*

TRIO

SIR HUON:	And must I then dissemble?
FATIMA:	No other hope I know—
SIR HUON:	But let the tyrant tremble– Unscathed he shall not go!
FATIMA:	Viewless spirit of pow'r and light! Thou who mak'st virtue and love thy care, Restore to the best and the bravest knight The fondest and fairest of the fair!
ALL:	Spirit adored! Strike on our part! Bless the good sword, And the faithful heart!

Scene II

An apartment in the haram of the Emir.

Enter ALMANZOR, *followed by a Black Slave.*

ALMANZOR: Has the lovely stranger been refreshed and habited, as we
commanded?

SLAVE: The will of my lord has been faithfully executed by his slave.

ALMANZOR: Conduct her hither. (*Exit Slave.*) Yes – I will again behold
those eyes, dark and tender as the mountain roe's; again listen to
that voice, sweet as the breeze-rung bells of Paradise! Thrice blessed
be the waves which flung her back upon that desert shore! They
cover not so fair a pearl, they never bore a richer treasure. She
comes! – she comes! – Unseen, awhile I'll gaze upon her beauty;
then pay a prince's tribute to its power! (*Retires.*)

Enter REIZA, *richly habited.*

SONG

REIZA:　Mourn thou, poor heart, for the joys that are dead;
　　　　Flow, ye sad tears, for the hopes that are fled:
　　　　Sorrow is now the sole treasure I prize;
　　　　As Peris on perfume, I feed on its sighs:
　　　　And bitter to some as its fountain may be,
　　　　'Tis sweet as the waters of Gelum to me.*

　　　　Ye that are basking in Pleasure's gay beam,
　　　　Ye that are sailing on Hope's golden stream,
　　　　A cloud may come o'er ye – a wave sweep the deck,
　　　　And picture a future of darkness and wreck;
　　　　But the scourge of the desert† o'er *my* heart *hath* past,
　　　　And the tree that *is* blighted fears no *second* blast.

ALMANZOR (*advancing*):　Beautiful being! wherefore that plaintive lay,
sweet and sad as the moan of the dove over the fallen cypress? –
Tell me thy grief, that I may bring to thee the balm will cure it. –
Almanzor can do much.

REIZA:　Can he awake the dead?

ALMANZOR:　No – but he can surround the living with such delights
that they will weep the dead no longer.

REIZA:　Indeed! Then waste them not on me – for I would still weep
on. – My hopes have passed from me, like the phantom streams
which mock the fainting traveller in the desert; and, like him, would
I lay me down and die.

ALMANZOR:　Hath Almanzor then no power to bid a spring gush forth
for thee in the wilderness? Is there no green oasis to which his hand
may lead thee? Bethink thee, loveliest, – all that charmeth woman,
– gay chambers, – costly robes, – high feasting, and sweet music,
these are mine to offer thee, and –

REIZA:　All these I had, and I left them without a sigh! Without a sigh
I can remember that I had them. They increased not my happiness
when I *was* happy, and they can take no jot from my wretchedness!
– A costly robe but adds to the weight of a sinking spirit; and when
the nightingale is dead, and the canker in the heart of the rose, she
careth not for the smile of the sun, or the song of the fountain.

ALMANZOR:　Hear me, fair creature! I know not whom thou art, or
whence thou comest, beyond what they could tell, who brought
thee hither! – But this I know, thy beauty is above all price. The
caliph, my great master, before whom the whole world falls pros-
trate, should not buy thee from me! – Nay, by Allah! if rank and
power can move thy heart to love, speak but the word, I will fling
off allegiance, defy Haroun, and share with thee the independent
throne of Tunis.

---

　* 'The water of Gelum, on account of its purity, is called the water of
Paradise.' Dow.
　† The kamsin, a devastating wind so called by the Arabs.

REIZA: Dream it not! – Almanzor, there is a gulf between us: its dark shore is strewed with the wreck of happiness: come not thou near it with thy gilded bark, if thou wouldst save thyself.

ALMANZOR: Thou art Almanzor's sovereign; but yet hear me. Thy grief shall be respected: no boisterous mirth shall break its spell, – no rude intrusion profane its sanctuary; but gentlest cares shall daily steal away some unmarked portion of thy melancholy, till the light of joy may pierce its last thin shadow. – Nay, reply not! – For thine own sake, do not wake me from this vision, even though it be delusive. Leave me, while yet I feel myself thy slave. A moment longer, and I may remember I am also thy master.

(*Exit* REIZA.)

As ALMANZOR *is rushing out on the opposite side, enter* ROSHANA.

ALMANZOR: Roshana!

ROSHANA: Light of my eyes! what shakes my lord so strongly: – your cheek is flushed, your look is wild, Almanzor – Why do you frown on me? – have I offended?

ALMANZOR: Your sight offends me – stand from out my path.

ROSHANA: The emir of Tunis was not wont to speak thus to Roshana. The blood of the Prophet runs in these veins; let my lord shed it, but not insult his wife.

ALMANZOR: My wife! my slave! By Allah, one word more, and Tunis shall not hold a slave so wretched as I will make the proud Roshana. Out of my path, before I spurn thee! Hence, and vent thy spleen upon thy women; but for thy life, wake not Almanzor's fury!

(*Exit* ALMANZOR.)

ROSHANA: O holy Prophet! why have I lived to see this day? – Why *do* I live to bear this foul disgrace. – Why, but for vengeance! Yes, by Allah! terrible vengeance! Cast off, – despised, – insulted, – for this new toy, – this pining stranger. – Roshana, awake! Hast thou no power in Tunis? – Yes, today. – But wilt thou have tomorrow? Not if this minion listen to the suit of thy faithless lord. Well then, today, while I have power, let me use it. – Her vengeance glutted, Roshana knows how to die, and foil that of her enemies.

(*Exit.*)

Scene III

Myrtle grove in the garden of ALMANZOR.

Enter FATIMA.

FATIMA: Well, that's settled: – our master the gardener has consented to employ our master the Paladin; and the latter has already commenced operations. Sherasmin told the old man a famous story about his sham kinsman's skill in raising tulips! – Heaven send he put it not to the proof, for there'll not be a plant left alive in the whole garden, I'm sure. – He doesn't know a tulip from a sunflower! He handles a hoe as if it were a lance, and slashes about with his pruning knife as tho' he were lopping heads instead of branches. – Hah! here he comes.

Enter SIR HUON, *dressed as a gardener, hastily: in his hand is a bouquet, which he examines minutely.*

SIR HUON: It must be from my Reiza! I've heard that in these climes, each flower hath a meaning, and that lovers often express their passionate thoughts in such sweet letters! O for some clue to read this riddle! (*Seeing* FATIMA.) Hah! Fatima! tell me, my kind girl, what may this mean? Standing but now, gazing upon the cruel walls which bar me from my Reiza, I saw the small fair hand of a female issue from the only lattice which opens on these gardens, – and presently this bunch of flowers fell from it at my feet.

(Giving them to her.)

FATIMA: Ha! they are token flowers. A Turkish girl taught me to read such riddles. (*Examining the bouquet, and explaining its meaning to* SIR HUON.) See, my lord, a jonquil, – that means 'Have pity on my passion.' These cinnamon blossoms, – 'My fortune is yours.' – Stay, what is this? – these flowers puzzle me – I have it – no – I cannot make that out. The gold wire that binds them should mean, 'I die for thee – come quickly!' – And look – here are some characters scratched upon this laurel leaf, – 'At sunset, the gate in the myrtle grove – love, and vengeance on a tyrant.' It's from my lady, – she has doubtless gained some slave, who will direct your steps to her; but ah! the danger.

SIR HUON: Talk not of danger in a cause like this! Hasten to Sherasmin: tell him to prepare for instant flight. – Day is closing fast and there is no time for consultation. Do thou and he await me at the well behind the gardener's house. There, if fate smile upon my enterprise, will I bring thy mistress.

FATIMA: And if fate does *not* smile upon us, tomorrow morning will find Sherasmin and I at the bottom of the well; for never will we outlive the loss of our dear lord and lady.

(Exit FATIMA.)

SIR HUON: At sunset! the gate in the myrtle grove! 'Tis here at hand, and the moment is almost as nigh. My own true Reiza! A few brief seconds, and I shall clasp her again to this devoted bosom.

SONG

SIR HUON: I revel in hope and joy again;
            A ray shines over my breaking chain,
            Beams like a beacon the gloom above,
            And lights my path to my lady love!

            I feel like a mountain stream set free
            From the stern frost-spirit's mastery,
            Rushing down from its rocky height,
            Leaping and sparkling in wild delight.

I revel in hope and joy again!
I seek my love as that stream the main:
They shall turn the tide with a silken glove,
Ere they bar my way to my lady love!

Scene IV

Saloon in the kiosk of ROSHANA: *in the flat an arch closed with rich curtains.
The stage is quite dark.*

Enter NADINA, *leading* SIR HUON.

SIR HUON: Where is she? Gentle guide – where is my love?

NADINA: Rest thou here – anon thou shalt behold her.

(Exit NADINA.)

SIR HUON: My heart misgives me! – why this strange delay: – the
passage was free for her as for the slave, and by this time we should
have joined our friends. She comes not – how torturing is this
suspense!

The curtains of the arch fly open and discover a recess illuminated, in which
ROSHANA *is reclining, covered with a rich veil.*

Ah! she is there! My love! my life! (*Rushing to her, and clasping her in
his arms.*) Why dost thou loiter here? Let us away! the morn shall
see us far from Tunis!

ROSHANA (*throwing off her veil*):   Nay, Christian, not so. The morn
shall see thee on the throne of Tunis, if thou wilt share it with
Roshana!

SIR HUON: Merciful heaven! I am betrayed!

ROSHANA: Thou hast no cause for fear: – listen to me, Christian. Thou
seest before thee the wife of Almanzor, the proud emir of Tunis. I
mark'd thee toiling in the garden beneath the eye of Ibrahim, and
could see thy spirit spurned the menial task. Thou art no common
slave – there is a fire in thine eye, a pride in thy port, which speak
thee noble: – suffice it to say, I saw and loved thee. – Let not thy
colder nature start at this plain avowal. – The passions of the daughters of Africa burn as fiercely as the sun which blazes over them.
Two of the wildest now rage within my bosom – vengeance and
love. Nerve thine arm, Christian, to gratify the first – the latter shall
reward thee beyond thy most sanguine wishes!

SIR HUON (*aside*):   Whither hath my rashness led me? How shall I
answer this impetuous woman?

KOSHANA: Thou art silent. Canst thou hesitate to accept the good I
offer thee? – Arouse thee, Christian. Is it not thy glory to smite the
Muslim? Listen – I will lead thee this night to the couch of Almanzor.
When his brain swims with the forbidden wine, and his lids are
heavy with the fumes of the banquet, stab him to the heart! His
slaves shall fall like dust at thy feet. The harem yields obedience to
my nod. Wealth, rank, and power – liberty and love – reward thee
for one blow!

SIR HUON: Never, mighty princess! If Almanzor has wronged thee, give me a sword, and let me hand to hand strive with the tyrant! I will shed my blood freely to right an injured woman; but I am no assassin to stab a sleeping man!

ROSHANA: Is he not the enemy of thy race and creed? Must the lances glitter in the sun, and the mighty steed paw up the earth before thy blood can boil and thy steel spring from its scabbard? Think on thy countrymen who pine in chains around thee, and nourish with the sweat of their brows the soil of the infidel! Thou shalt be their liberator, and I will be thy proselyte! Thou shalt have the glory of giving freedom to five hundred Franks, and of converting a princess of the blood of Mohammed! What care I for a prince who spurns me, or a Prophet who denies me the privileges of my fellow clay? Christian! gallant Christian! revenge thyself and me – strike the tyrant and the unbeliever, and defy the caliph on his distant throne.

SIR HUON: Urge me no more, lady. I love another; and while I freely own thy dazzling beauty, and my unworthiness, I must declare as plainly, that naught can shake my honour or my faith.

ROSHANA (aside):   Destruction to my hopes! Wretched Roshana! where is the boasted power of thine eyes? where are the charms that poets have sung, and princes have sighed for? A slave, whose life hangs on thy breath, calmly rejects thine hand, even with a jewell'd sceptre in its grasp! – But shall this be? shall I be baffled thus? Come all ye arts of woman to my aid! the touch that disarms the mighty – the look that blinds the wise! He must be more or less than man if he break through the net I cast around him.

She claps her hands. – A troop of dancing girls and female slaves, richly attired, enter and surround SIR HUON *with garlands. One presents him with a cup of wine.*

GRAND SCENA AND CHORUS

Chorus

SIR HUON, &c.:
>   For thee hath beauty decked her bower,
>   For thee the cup of joy is filled:
>   O drain the draught and cull the flower,
>   Ere the rose be dead and the wine be spilled!

Solo

SIR HUON: Hence! The flow'rs ye proffer fair,
>   Poison in their fragrance bear!
>   And the goblet's purple flood
>   Seems to me a draught of blood!

He breaks from the garlands, and is met by ROSHANA, *who clings to him and prevents his flight.*

Chorus

>   When woman's eye with love is bright,
>   Canst thou shun its 'witching light?

Bearest thou the heart to flee
When her white arms circle thee?

Solo

SIR HUON:

There is no beauty in woman's eye,
When it burns with unholy brilliancy!
'Tis like the glare of the sightless dead,
When the soul which should kindle their orbs hath fled!

There is no charm that can yield delight
In the wanton's hand, be it never so white –
Sooner its fingers should o'er me stray,
When the worm hath eaten the flesh away!

Disengages himself from ROSHANA, *and rushes to the wing by which he entered. – The dancing girls and slaves anticipate his intention, and group themselves so as to oppose his exit.*

Chorus

O turn not away from the banquet of bliss!
O lose not a moment so precious as this!
Remember the sage★ who sang o'er his repast
'How pleasant were life, if a shadow could last.'
Then, mortal, be happy, and laugh at the wise
Who know life's a shadow, yet wait till it flies!

SIR HUON: Off! let me pass. I would not willingly lay an ungentle hand upon a woman, but patience hath its bounds! Give way, I say!

As he is about to force his way through them the slaves disperse, and ALMANZOR *enters, followed by some armed Negroes.* SIR HUON *is instantly seized.*

ALMANZOR: Eternal curses! a man within these walls.

ROSHANA (*aside*):   Almanzor! flushed with wine too – 'tis well, the slave shall die the death his folly merits! (*Aloud, and falling at* ALMANZOR's *feet.*) Allah be praised! I owe thee more than life! This Christian dog, for some vile purpose, and by unknown means, gained access to this sacred spot. My slaves discovered him, and he would have fled. Shrieking, they strove with their weak arms to bar his passage; when happily my lord arrived, as sent by heaven to our assistance!

ALMANZOR: Drag him away to death. In the palace court let him be burned alive, within this hour! (*They force* SIR HUON *from the stage.*) Woman (*to* ROSHANA), I doubt this tale, but be it as it may, he dies! For thee – (*Pauses awhile and observes her: then, turning to one of the remaining Negroes, he silently motions him towards* ROSHANA.)

ROSHANA (*aside*):   Hah! is it so? There is no time to lose then.

As two of the Negroes approach her, she evades their grasp; and rushing on

★ Abdolmélik, the fifth caliph of the house of Ommiyah, and the eleventh from the Prophet: whilst he was at supper, he said, 'How sweetly we live, if a shadow would last!'

vide Oakley's *Hist. of the Saracens*

ALMANZOR *aims a blow at him with her dagger: her arm is caught, and the weapon wrested from her, by a third slave.*

ALMANZOR (*in a calm low tone*): Thou hast been dangerous too long. Farewell, Roshana. Thine is a towering spirit, but the Tigris is deep enough to cover it.

ROSHANA (*in the same tone*): Were it as deep as Gehennem, it should not separate us, Almanzor. In the banquet hall and the haram bower, in the blaze of noon and the darkness of night, Roshana shall be with thee, her blue lip shall meet thine on the brim of the goblet, her glassy eye glare on thee from the midst of the roses. The rushing of waters and the shriek of their victim shall be heard above the song of joy and the trumpet of triumph. Sleeping and waking shall they ring in thine ears; and when the angel of death shall stand at the foot of thy couch, there shall Roshana be also, to smile on the last struggle of her despairing murderer!

ALMANZOR *signs to the Negroes to remove* ROSHANA. *The scene closes.*

Scene V

Garden behind IBRAHIM's *house – a rose-bush particularly prominent. – Moonlight.*

Enter SHERASMIN.

SHERASMIN: No, I can see nobody. Mischief! mischief! I greatly fear thou art afoot! My master must have been here long ago, had he succeeded in his project! If they have discovered him, they'll twist his neck with as little compunction as if it were a pigeon's! Fatima returns not, neither! Has she heard nothing? Or has she heard too much? Sir Oberon! Sir Oberon! I begin to fear that thou will turn out a scurvy fairy, after all. – O murder! what the devil's that? I've trode on a snake, and it has bitten my leg through! O! I'm a dead man! (*A lily rises through the stage, and the ivory horn is seen swinging upon it.*) There it is! – No – it isn't – It's a – no – why – (*Approaching cautiously, and looking at it.*) The horn! the horn! the fairy horn! (*Snatching it from the lily, which sinks again, and dancing about delightedly.*) We're all right! we're all safe – we're all – Lira, lira la! lira, lira la! Ah, Fatima!

Enter FATIMA, *hastily.*

FATIMA: Misery! misery! all's lost! all's ruined! We were deceived! The token came from the wife of the emir! Almanzor surprised Sir Huon in the harem, and they are going to burn him alive!

SHERASMIN: Burn him alive! – My master – ha! ha! ha! that's a good joke!

FATIMA: A good joke! art thou mad? I tell thee even now they are raising stake and pile in the court of the haram.

SHERASMIN: Excellent! 'twill be rare sport – follow me, Fatima!

FATIMA: He's frantic! the dreadful tidings have turned his brain.

SHERASMIN: No, they hav'n't. Don't be frighten'd. If I am mad, I'm only horn-mad, and that's nothing very extraordinary for a married man, you know, Fatima.

FATIMA: What! the fairy horn restored to us? But are you sure it's the fairy horn? It may be some trick, perhaps.

SHERASMIN: Sure! why, – yes, – it must be – it – at least, it looks very much like it. – (*Blows a soft note.* FATIMA *bursts into a loud laugh.*) Oh yes. I can swear to the notes – come – come, don't stand laughing there – every moment is precious now.

FATIMA: Oh! oh! oh! ha! ha! I can't help it! ha! ha! ha!

SHERASMIN: What the deuce ails the girl! Fatima! – Fatima! – Oh murder! it's the horn – that's for doubting the fairy, you know – what's to be done now? – If I blow again, I shall do more mischief. – So, you must e'en laugh on, till I get within hearing of the enemy, and then take your chance with the rest. – Follow me, you grinning goose, do – 'Guienne for the noble duke!'

FATIMA: Ha! ha! ha!

(*Exeunt* – FATIMA *laughing.*)

Scene VI

The court of the haram. In the centre of the stage is a stake, surrounded by faggots. A band of Negroes are discovered, with lighted torches.

Enter ALMANZOR, *attended.*

ALMANZOR: Bring forth the guilty slave!

(*Exeunt Negroes.*)

A shriek is heard within: REIZA *rushes from the harem, and flings herself at the feet of* ALMANZOR.

The lovely stranger!

REIZA: At thy feet, Almanzor, I crave a first and only boon.

ALMANZOR: What canst thou ask, fair creature, that Almanzor can deny? Speak; it is thine.

REIZA: Pardon for him thou hast but now condemned to a most cruel and unmerited death.

ALMANZOR: How! for that vile slave who dared profane the harem! What is that dog to thee?

REIZA: He was deceived, and he is innocent. I have heard all. Ask thine own slaves, the slaves of that wretched princess now struggling with the waters of the Tigris. Spare him! O spare him!

ALMANZOR: It cannot be! He hath transgressed the law. Waste not a thought upon a wretch like that.

REIZA: Almanzor, hear me – he is my husband.

ALMANZOR: Hah! thy husband! He whom thy captors left bound upon the beach, and thou didst dèem dead? Praised be the Prophet! Now, lady, hear Almanzor; you ask me to be merciful – do thou set the example. Pity *my* sufferings, smile upon my love; and I will not only spare his life, but load him with riches, and give him safe and honourable conduct to his native land.

REIZA (*rising*): Never!

ALMANZOR: Beware! the bow, o'erstrained, may break.

REIZA: Barbarian, do thy worst; I fear thee not. The man I love would shame to live on terms so base; and I would rather share his dreadful fate, than free him from it by such infamy.

ALMANZOR (*furiously*): Then be it so. Thou hast condemned thyself; for yield thou shalt, or mount the pile with him. Bind her to the stake, and bring the Christian forth.

(*Slaves seize and bind* REIZA.)

Negroes enter with SIR HUON.

SIR HUON: Reiza! O heavy hour!

REIZA: O happy hour! Huon, we die together.

ALMANZOR: Enough! To the stake with them, and fire the pile!

REIZA (*as they are dragging him to the stake*): Tyrant, beware! Thou killest the caliph's daughter; Haroun will rend thee piecemeal.

ALMANZOR (*laughing scornfully*): Ha! ha! ha! that lie will scarcely serve thy turn. But, were it true, she hath wedded with a vile Christian, and deserves to die. Slaves, fire the pile, I say!

As the Negroes are about to set fire to the pile, the faint sound of a horn is heard. ALMANZOR *becomes motionless. – The Negroes and other slaves dance to the following chorus.*

FINALE

CHORUS: Hark! what notes are swelling?
　　　　Whence that wondrous sound,
　　　Ev'ry note compelling
　　　　In merry dance to bound?

Enter ARCON, *and* SHERASMIN *with the horn, followed by* FATIMA.

Quartetto

SIR HUON, REIZA, SHERASMIN and FATIMA:
　　　Rejoice! Rejoice! 'tis the horn of power!
　　　They dance in the court and they dance in the tower!
　　　They dance in the garden, they dance in the hall,
　　　On the ocean beach and the city wall.
　　　A second and louder blast shall bring
　　　The donor himself – the elfin king!

SHERASMIN *blows a louder blast; the bonds of* SIR HUON *and* REIZA *are burst asunder; the faggots and stake sink. – The stage fills with clouds as in Act II. The Negroes and* ALMANZOR *fly in terror.*

The clouds open: OBERON *and* TITANIA *appear.*

Recitative

OBERON: Hail, faithful pair! your woes are ended!
　　　Your friend in turn you have befriended!
　　　His pledge redeemed by you hath been;
　　　Again in love he clasps his fairy queen!

Air

Swift as the lightning's glance,
  Brave knight, behold, I bring
Thee and thine to thy native France,
And the palace of thy king.
Kneel at his feet with the bride thou hast won;
Europe shall ring with the deed thou hast done:
Now for ever I break the spell
With the grateful fairy's last farewell.

The clouds envelope OBERON *and* TITANIA, *then rise and discover the Palace of* CHARLEMAGNE. – *Grand march. Enter guards, nobles and ladies of the Emperor's court, and lastly* CHARLEMAGNE. *He ascends the throne. Flourish.*

SIR HUON, REIZA, SHERASMIN *and* FATIMA, *who have left the stage at the change of scene, re-enter,* SIR HUON *armed as in first scene. He leads* REIZA *to the foot of the throne. – They kneel.*

Recitative

SIR HUON:

Behold! Obedient to the oath he swore,
Huon is kneeling at thy feet once more.
For, by the help of heaven, his hand hath done
The daring deed, and from the caliph won
This lovely maid, – by ev'ry peril tried,
The heiress of his throne, and now thy vassal's bride.

CHARLEMAGNE *raises and welcomes* SIR HUON *and* REIZA.

CHORUS

Hail to the knight with his own good brand,
Who hath won a fair bride from the Saracen's hand!
Hail to the maiden, who over the sea
Hath followed her champion so faithfully!
By bards yet unborn oft' the tale shall be told
Of Reiza the lovely and Huon the bold!